Thomas S. Heemstra

ANTHRAX

A DEADLY
SHOT
IN THE DARK

Unmasking the Truth
Behind a Hazardous Vaccine

CRYSTAL
COMMUNICATIONS

Crystal Communications
2009 Family Circle, Suite 3
Lexington, KY 40505
Phone: (859) 255-0076
Fax: (859) 255-0938
Email: crystalky@starband.net

Printed in the United States of America

Edited by Bobbie Newman and Christine Clough
Cover and text design by Todd W. Detering

First printing: February 2002

Library of Congress Catalog Card Number: 20-02100952

ISBN: 0-945738-53-6

To my father, Ronald E. Heemstra, who taught me love, discipline, generosity, an excellent work ethic, and the courage to stand up for what is right.

And to the late Colonel ("Dad") Robert J. Segars, U.S. Air Force (Retired), who served our country with excellence, integrity, and professionalism.

They planted the seeds of courage in my life and nurtured them with love through their example. I salute them with the deepest respect and admiration.

Abbreviations

AVA . . . . .Anthrax Vaccine Adsorbed
AVIP . . . . .Anthrax Vaccine Immunization Program
CANG . . . . .Connecticut Air National Guard
CBER . . . . .Center for Biologics Evaluation and Research
CDC . . . . .Center for Disease Control
CGMP . . . . .Current Good Manufacturing Practice
DARPA . . . . .Defense Acquisition Research Project Agency
FDA . . . . .Food and Drug Administration
GAO . . . . .General Accounting Office
GWI . . . . .Gulf War illness
HEW . . . . .U.S. Department of Health, Education, and Welfare
HGRC . . . . .House Government Reform Committee
IND . . . . .Investigational New Drug
IOM . . . . .Institute of Medicine
JVAP . . . . .Joint Vaccination Acquisition Program
MBPI . . . . .Michigan Biological Products Institute—BioPort
MDPH . . . . .Michigan Department of Public Health—BioPort
MOU . . . . .Memorandum of Understanding
NIH . . . . .National Institute of Health
SAIC . . . . .Science Applications International Corporation
SASC . . . . .Senate Armed Services Committee
UCMJ . . . . .Uniform Code of Military Justice
USAFA . . . . .United States Air Force Academy
USAMRIID . . . . . .United States Army Medical Research Institute
of Infectious Diseases
VAERS . . . . .Vaccine Adverse Event Reporting System

Table of Contents

DISCLAIMER: *This book is not intended in any way to offer medical advice. Consult your physician before making any personal medical decisions.*

Acknowledgments

Thank you, Bobbie Newman and Christine Clough, for your outstanding editorial skills and patience throughout this project. Thanks also to Todd Detering and Irv Trachtenberg for your special contributions. And to conclude recognition for Crystal Communications, thank you, Ed Puterbaugh, for your leadership, passion, and professional expertise to make it happen. You all are the best!

Special thanks to Alise and Jason, Becky and Renae, for the love and inspiration you bring to my life.

I want to express my deep admiration and appreciation for the men and women around this country, both military and civilian, who have invested countless hours in the battle against this hazardous vaccine. Together, this group salutes our armed forces, desiring to leave a legacy of integrity and accountability that is desperately needed for our future.

Specifically, I want to applaud Dr. Meryl Nass and Dr. Pam Asa for their medical expertise, professionalism, and treatment offered to many of the victims of this vaccine. I commend Major Tom "Buzz" Rempfer and Major Russ Dingle, the two Connecticut Air National Guard pilots who began this battle; they will continue their search for the truth and see it through to the end. Without their research efforts and persistence, this battle would not be possible. And deep admiration goes to Colonel (Retired) Redmond Handy for his leadership, exhaustive research, and writing. Redmond is the president of NO ABUSE, National Organization of Americans Battling Unnecessary Servicemember Endangerment, a tax-exempt charity.

J.R. Richardson, Major Sonnie Bates, and Captain John Buck also deserve special recognition for their contributions, courage under fire, and patriotism.

Thank you to the many U.S. Congress members and staff for their leadership and personal assistance in supporting and giving a voice to the men and women of the armed forces. Congressmen Shays, Burton, Fletcher, Metcalf, Sanders, Jones, Souder, and Gilman stand out for their contributions and concern.

FOREWORD

The House Government Reform Subcommittee on National Security, Veterans Affairs, and International Relations, which I chair, has held hearings on a wide range of issues, including the Department of Defense's forcewide Anthrax Vaccine Immunization Program (AVIP), Gulf War illness, and vulnerabilities to waste, fraud, and abuse in the Departments of Defense and Veterans Affairs. I met Lieutenant Colonel Tom Heemstra when he testified before the Subcommittee in September 1999.

The men and women who serve our country defending freedom deserve to be treated with nothing less than the highest level of dignity and respect and to be equipped with the best resources. The vaccine chosen to meet the serious biological threat of anthrax should be as well-tested and as technologically advanced as the F-16 Tom flew. Instead, the current vaccine is dated medical technology, difficult to administer, and is known to cause adverse reactions.

As a result, the plan to vaccinate all military personnel against anthrax threatens to erode the very military readiness it is designed to protect.

When the troops needed an advocate and the vaccine victims needed a voice, when honor was challenged and truth was in jeopardy, Tom answered the call, knowing that the stakes could be high. This story is one of courage, selflessness, and patriotism.

Tom's message is articulate, inspirational, and on target. His devotion and persistence in unmasking the truth gives the American public confidence that the military is producing the highest standard in leaders. The bittersweet irony of Tom's forced retirement does not inhibit his ongoing efforts to protect the health of millions.

The Honorable Christopher Shays
Member of Congress
Connecticut 4th District

Introduction

The Basis and the Background

Our minds possess by nature an insatiable desire to know the truth.
—Cicero

Never in the field of human conflict was so much owed by so many to so few.
—Sir Winston Churchill

The Basis

In the aftermath of September 11, and now in the midst of the War on Terrorism, we are stunned by the numbers: "Five Dead, Dozens Injured from Terrorist Anthrax Attack."

But the headline that the media is missing is even more alarming: "Six Dead, Thousands Injured from the Anthrax Vaccine." The release of that news story would report the balance of truth critically important for all Americans today.

Before the September 11 terrorist attacks and the anthrax incidents that followed, few Americans understood what anthrax was. Even fewer were aware that for years, their nation's 2.4 million soldiers, airmen, and marines have faced, and continue to face, a potentially dangerous—and mandatory—vaccine. Now, the anthrax vaccine controversy invades every home with startling relevancy, because terrorism has proved that it is possible to deliver the anthrax threat directly to our mailboxes.

Dying for You to Know

Many civilians and military personnel are literally dying for you to know about this vaccine. Some have sacrificed careers and financial security. Some have sacrificed their health and are gravely ill. Lives have already been lost. Many others have sold their souls, sacrificing truth and their personal integrity on the career altar.

The military began mandatory anthrax vaccine inoculations for everyone in uniform in May 1998. This policy was called the Anthrax Vaccine Immunization Program, or AVIP. All 2.4 million troops were slated to take the shot by 2005. The truth, however, is that the anthrax vaccine is untested, the production of it is unlawful, the administration of it is unethical, and the vaccine itself is unsafe.

Not just civilians are unaware; the troops themselves were not adequately informed about the shot, especially those on active duty. Some chose to look the other way, satisfied to accept claims by what turned out to be a government and military policy gone astray. Others simply were not given a reliable source of information.

Now that anthrax has become a household word, perhaps it is not too late to change course and to prevent the deadly results of the military's anthrax shot policy before it becomes recommended public policy. By mid-October 2001, more than 1,200 people had already called BioPort, the manufacturer of the vaccine, to see how they could get vaccinated. Panic is outpacing common sense or knowledge about the shot.

Why This Book and Why Now?

During a period spanning 1999 and 2000, the Government Reform Committee of the United States House of Representatives (HGRC) held nine hearings, resulting in the publication of a 100-page report entitled *Unproven Force Protection.* The conclusion and recommendation was that the AVIP should be suspended because it lacks an essential element in a medical program: trust.[1]

The events of 2001, a new presidential administration, and the terrorist anthrax attack are all factors that contribute to this program's continuation. If those in leadership turn a blind eye and allow the program to continue, the public clamor for a vaccine may bring this threat to the doorstep of a vulnerable, uninformed, and unsuspecting public.

This book is meant to inform you of the background and dangers of the anthrax vaccine. Education is critical. Over the past few years, the military has unexpectedly, with little preparation time or facts available, had to face this predicament. All of a sudden, postal workers, congressional staffers, and media members who may have been exposed to poisonous anthrax must decide whether to risk taking the vaccine. Tomorrow you could face the same decision. Where will the next terrorist anthrax attack occur? Your civilian leaders suggest "not if, but when?" In this case, what you don't know will hurt you.

This book was not written to provide specific medical advice to you or to recommend that you not take the shot. However, I implore you to make an educated and informed decision, knowing and comprehending the risks. Understand the effects of the vaccine in the lives of many victims you haven't heard about until now. My hope is that you will benefit from their stories and from this investigation, and that you will make a decision that fits your perspective of safety and security.

This book does not advocate disobeying military orders. Doing so could place one in great peril and one's career in immediate jeopardy. Although there is room in the military for the officer corps and decision makers to question the legality of orders, the decision to refuse the vaccine cannot be made lightly. It involves a summation and continuous evaluation of all the principles that are precious to us: patriotism, loyalty, commitment, love for humanity, freedom, duty, honor, and country. It requires tedious research, legal knowledge, and expertise, plus a reservoir of moral fiber that allows the questioning of every premise and seeks satisfactory answers that uphold unwavering principles. Finally, it requires a willingness to sacrifice personal joy, pride, and accomplishment for a higher cause. Do not tread down this road lightly. Move cautiously, with respect and reverence for all you hold dear.

For me, that meant protecting those I served in my command position, not just the troops under my command, but also you as an American citizen. I swore to protect and defend both, "against all enemies, foreign and domestic."

Initially, this book was written to inform and protect the military. However, in light of recent events, it is critical to prevent civilians from being victimized as well.

I know the men and women who have become victims; there have already been too many personal tragedies. I also know many in the military who stay sick silently for fear of losing their jobs, their livelihoods, their family security. Some are so sick that their lives are changed forever. They have daily reminders in the medicine that they are sentenced to take. Some have not even told family members that they took the vaccine, fearing the turmoil and instability that an illness will cause for their families. Some part-time military members won't tell their civilian full-time employers of their serious ongoing symptoms from this mandatory military vaccination program, fearing the loss of income, job security, and health care benefits.

Fortunately, others freely tell their stories here, having lost all fear. Braving the future and facing one day at a time, they want you to know. I hoped to prevent this hardship and to protect each of them. We worked hard, trying to keep anyone else from joining the victims list. Many military members sacrificed careers. As an F-16 Fighter Squadron Commander, I tried my best both to protect my troops and to prevent future victims, some friends, some nameless. I sacrificed my career in the process, and it's important that I share that story, too, to keep others from facing the same end.

It is critical that the damaged are repaired and that amends are made. Those who are sick need medical diagnosis and treatment. Resources must be made available to help them recover, physically, mentally, and emotionally. Because of the vaccine controversy, many careers were ended prematurely, either by court-martial or forced resignations and transfers. Many of these service members were war veterans. Reparations should be made, and invitations to serve their nation should be extended without malice. Finally, the process must be modified to ensure that we do not repeat the same mistakes with future vaccines and to ensure that we restore trust in the system and in our military leadership as they develop effective force protection. This book is a starting point.

Help Is Needed

Doing all this requires your help. Your involvement is needed to defend the military that has so proudly served and defended you and your homeland, both in the past and today, fighting terrorism around the world. Their health and safety is at risk from the AVIP. As military personnel, they are in a difficult position—they must defend their own human rights against internal threats from home while they are battling for your rights and those of others on distant shores. Once you are informed, become involved, for their sakes as well as your own.

You may have to face the same decision, whether to take the shot and risk your and your family's health, based on U.S. Department of Defense recommendations, or whether to speak out and demand safety, accountability, and a quality vaccine. Postal workers are facing the vaccine decision now; next, it may be your turn.

It's vital to know what you are about to inject into your body. As an F-16 fighter pilot, I often used the term "check six" to ensure that pilots visually clear their rear quadrants of all potential enemy aircraft from a sneak attack. Before taking the anthrax shot in your arm or your backside, check six. Know the threat and know the vaccine. Don't be caught off guard. Civilians can do much more and more quickly than military personnel to demand higher quality standards. The military is being forced to settle for less. Demand that the government offer a safe and effective vaccine to you and to your military.

Together, let's all check six. This book will help you begin by presenting six sinister characteristics of the anthrax vaccine immunization program: AVIP is untested, unsafe, unnecessary, unpopular, unethical, and unlawful. In the final pages, we bring you the latest updates on this uncontrolled vaccine.

The Background

Victims of the Anthrax Vaccine Immunization Program (AVIP) are becoming more vocal and gaining confidence as their numbers increase, but unfortunately, their symptoms continue to get worse. Many of their stories speak volumes from these pages. Hear their pleas and avoid their fate.

Initially, these victims hoped that telling their stories would help protect others in the military. Most had not dreamed of how their stories and their efforts would also help civilians. But in the aftermath of September 11, 2001, this is a serious, deadly, urgent issue for everyone. If you are faced with taking the shot as a military member, or now as a postal worker, federal employee, or intern in Washington, D.C., or as a civilian, this story has immediate impact on your future health and safety. Why all the buzz? The commotion centers on the search for sufficient and satisfactory answers.

Is the anthrax vaccine safe? It's tested and proven, right? Should people get the protection, however minimal, that a vaccine might offer? Can vaccines provide protection in a biological weapon attack? Don't most military members want the shot? Soldiers can't be allowed to question every order, can they? The short answer to all these questions is no. The longer, more detailed answers will follow.

What about those shot-dodgers? Aren't volunteers in the military required to follow orders and take the shot? The short answer is yes. The long answer is much more complicated. Officers and commanders have an obligation and command responsibility for the welfare of their troops and are bound only to obey lawful orders. They are, in fact, legally liable if they obey unlawful orders.

What's so controversial about the vaccine that military officers and enlisted personnel risk court-martial to disobey an order to take it? The AVIP presents a unique and unprecedented case study where military law and ethics, military strategy and personal safety, power, policy, and politics clash and combine in ways that encroach on our basic human rights and freedoms. The results and lessons learned are destined for the history books; they will shed light on the right way, and reveal the wrong way, to achieve military "force protection" in a biological warfare scenario of the twenty-first century.

An understanding of the disease anthrax and the origin of the vaccine are important for beginning your investigation. There is little disagreement on the disease types and treatment. But as soon as you begin researching the origin of the vaccine, you find stark controversy. This immediate split may explain the opposite poles, where the Defense Department finds itself in direct opposition to the majority of Americans and military troops at the grass-roots level who react unfavorably to the idea of taking the shot. This book explores the results of that crucial split and how it created an unacceptable vaccine policy.

What Is Anthrax?

Anthrax is a highly infectious disease caused by spores from a bacterium known as Bacillus anthracis.[2] Some believe that anthrax is described in the Bible as the second and fifth plagues in Exodus 8-9. Anthrax spores resist destruction, can lie dormant for centuries, and may be present in the soil for decades, infecting grazing animals that ingest the spores. Goats, sheep, and cattle are typically the animals that become infected.

In the past decade, there are years with no reported cases of human anthrax infection in the United States. Immunization of animals and people at risk has likely contributed to this decline. Third-world countries, especially agriculture-based economies, continue to report human anthrax cases. According to 2000-2001 data from the Centers for Disease Control and Prevention (CDC), approximately 130 cases of anthrax infection were reported in the United States per year.

Anthrax is not contracted from human to human. Human infection occurs by three methods of exposure to anthrax spores: cutaneous, gastrointestinal, and pulmonary.

Skin contact with live infected animals or with the hide, hair, or bones of an infected animal may lead to infection of a person's skin. This is known as cutaneous anthrax infection. This is the most common manifestation of anthrax in humans, accounting for more than 95 percent of cases. Untreated cutaneous anthrax has a death rate estimated at approximately 20 percent.

Eating undercooked or raw infected meat can cause gastrointestinal anthrax infection, deadly in 20 to 60 percent of cases.

Breathing in airborne spores may lead to pulmonary anthrax, which is also known as inhalation anthrax. Inhalation anthrax has a high mortality rate, 80 to 90 percent or higher. Those infected with inhalation anthrax usually die within a few days. Inhalation anthrax is the major threat that we should be concerned with. Inhalation anthrax infection has two phases. During the first phase, up to five days after inhalation of the spores, the patient has flulike symptoms, such as a cough, fatigue, and mild fever. Several days later, these symptoms may subside, but they are rapidly followed by the next, more severe state of the disease. During this phase, the patient experiences sudden onset of severe respiratory distress and even chest pain accompanied by fever. Chest x-rays may show fluid in the lungs. Within a day, septic shock and death will likely occur.

Antibiotics are the primary treatment for anthrax infection, but treatment has limited benefit unless given immediately after exposure. Just as vaccines are developed to combat diseases such as polio, smallpox, and even the flu, an effective anthrax vaccine was pursued. Louis Pasteur, Jean-Joseph Henri Toussaint, and W. S. Greenfield developed the first anthrax vaccines for animals around 1880. George Wright developed the first vaccine for humans at Fort Detrick in Maryland in the mid-1950s. The Defense Department owns the patent to the human vaccine, and it was first produced on a large scale by Merck & Co. Inc.

Two Vaccines

The first documented human use of the vaccine in the United States was in 1954, when it was administered to mill workers. When a study came out in 1962 on the vaccine's effects on the workers, the manufacturing process was changed, and the Michigan Department of Public Health (MDPH) took over production of the vaccine. This resulted in the existence of two vaccines made using different processes, creating a licensing nightmare that the Defense Department would rather ignore than explain.

In 1965, a patent was granted to the U.S. Army for what is called an anthrax "antigen" vaccine. On April 14, 1966, the CDC submitted an Investigational New Drug (IND) status for the anthrax vaccine to the Division of Biology, which was then part of the National Institute for Health and later transferred to the Food and Drug Administration (FDA). An application to license the vaccine was made in 1967. A study was conducted in Talladega, Alabama, using the patented vaccine. The original study of the antigen vaccine has never been documented, nor have the results been published. Most, if not all, other studies use the modified vaccine, not the one originally granted the license. The Division of Biologics, formerly the Public Health Service (the predecessor of the FDA), licensed this modified vaccine on November 10, 1970, for manufacturing by the MDPH.[3] The division would not have efficacy requirements for two more years. Despite the lack of efficacy testing, required or otherwise, the license was granted. All of these factors—the prolonged use, the lack of testing, and the unlicensed vaccine—all set the stage for controversy.

Critical to note is that the licensing procedure itself was fraught with error.

The fact is that two vaccines existed because they were made through different processes. The only legitimate license was granted for the original vaccine, before it was changed. The original vaccine's license is being illegally used for the second vaccine. The General Accounting Office (GAO) confirms in a report dated April 29, 1999, *Medical Readiness: Safety and Efficacy of the Anthrax Vaccine*, that the vaccine being administered by the Defense Department is not the same as the one originally tested prior to 1970.

The Defense Department does not typically acknowledge the existence of this second, different vaccine. It seems as if the Defense Department either does not grasp the significance and effects of early discrepancies in AVIP or that it sees them as something better off buried. So, while there is general agreement on the definition of anthrax, the story of the vaccine's origin changes depending on whether you are talking to the Defense Department or to another source.

Chapter 1 of this book presents details concerning the lack of testing by the Defense Department. In chapters 2 and 3, we explore how the Pentagon's policy, based on this already questionable foundation and lack of testing, yields undesirable results in terms of the overall safety and effectiveness seen in the implementation of the AVIP. Chapter 4 shows how unpopular the AVIP policy quickly became; early results had a significant impact on retention and morale. Chapters 5 and 6 examine how ethical and legal aspects of the Defense Department's actions combined to make the AVIP, from its very foundation, an unsound policy. Chapter 7 offers hope for a new beginning and a better way, with a call for accountability and responsibility. We end with an appendix of recommendations for both you and the government. Your participation is needed to protect your own health and that of the military who serve you. Armed with this knowledge, we can ensure that this program does not continue as the deadly and controversial guesswork that it is today.

A Deadly Shot in the Dark

"Deadly" speaks for itself from the headlines about those dead, dying, and injured from both anthrax infection and the vaccine. For those surprised by its outcome, the AVIP may best be summarized as an irresponsible guess. Through my studies and research, I have learned that the Defense Department's guess about the outcome was not as good as mine. The program was doomed from its poorly strategized beginning.

As an F-16 fighter pilot, I can imagine that developing this program must have been like being caught in a steep dive, screaming toward the ground at 600 miles per hour. At just a few thousand feet above the ground, you're not dead yet, but all that's left is for you to ride to the inevitable crash site -unless you eject. Then you can escape, with little more than wounded pride.

So why didn't the Defense Department just eject? Was it power, money, or institutional egomania? Surely, the department didn't want to relive the days when it was proven—and it admitted—that it turned military personnel into human guinea pigs for the so-called greater causes of radiation testing, LSD testing, and Agent Orange?

After you have read this book, your guess about the AVIP outcome will be as good as mine. The Defense Department would not say "your guess is as good as mine." For whatever reasons, military officials do not respond truthfully and forthrightly under oath; they are instructed to retain the attitude that "my guess is obviously better than yours." This became blazingly apparent, even as the hearings were conducted in the HGRC hearing room. The chairman, Congressman Dan Burton, had heard enough of the "canned answers" he received to each inquiry, and he finally slammed his microphone to the side in total frustration and disgust with the evasiveness of the military general's responses.

I shared those feelings of frustration, but they were mixed with embarrassment. The general being questioned represented the service to which I had dedicated most of my life. But the consequences of the AVIP—deaths, injuries, ruined careers, breakdown of trust in the military, and wasted taxpayer resources—only furthered my conviction that these issues needed to be brought to light.

It is disconcerting for Americans to see how the Defense Department has acted so irresponsibly, seemingly with no understanding or regard for the consequences of the AVIP. Perhaps the AVIP was well intentioned by some at the beginning, but it has grown out of control.

Fighting for Our Lives

Who has opposed this shot? Many victims and their families, several congressmen, the GAO, and several members of the military have exposed this program for the failure that it is. Many of them have been injured—mentally, emotionally, and physically—by the shot policy. Many careers of talented, skilled, and experienced military personnel have been lost; we need this experience and skill right now in our forces.

If only the American people knew. To date, media coverage has been lame, considering the risk that the AVIP poses to our military. Today's world requires policies that are above board, able to stand tough public scrutiny and rigid tests of integrity. From the inception of this mandatory shot program, and obvious to people who see this program at the grass-roots level, the truth has not been on the side of senior military leadership. This was evident in the testimonies of Defense Department senior officers before Congress, a frustration to our elected representatives. Our military leaders' careers are tied to a program, as one congressman suggested, rather than to the principles of integrity that have served many heroes before them. Rather than admit the truth about the unknowns and failures of this program, our military leaders will defend this program to its death. Hopefully, we will see that death in our lifetime. But we need your help.

This book informs you and issues a call for help from America's military. This book encourages critical, objective analysis. Don't blindly accept someone else's plan for you. Ask the right questions and demand satisfactory answers. This book unmasks the truth about the anthrax vaccine and the military policy—that it is untested, unsafe, unnecessary, unpopular, unwise, unethical, and unlawful, and uncontrolled.

This is a battle for truth, wisdom, accountability, and responsibility. This time, America's sons and daughters are counting on *you* to fight for them. Heaven forbid that this current vaccine is approved for public consumption. You are now in a battle to demand legal and ethical standards to protect yourself.

First, though, we need to know who is shooting. Who is the threat, and where is it coming from?

CHAPTER I

Friendly Fire

We have met the enemy and he is us.

—Pogo

Soldiers are citizens first; and whatever studies are formulated, they must be done with that concept in mind. Soldiers have the same constitutional rights as other citizens.

—Brigadier General Walter Busbee

An Untested Vaccine

In the summer of 1997, the 163rd Fighter Squadron deployed with our F-16s to Kuwait as part of Operation Desert Shield. Our surveillance mission was assigned to patrol the southern no-fly zone over Iraq. I flew fifteen combat sorties over Iraq in that three-week period. Fortunately, I never shot at anyone or dropped any bombs in anger during that postwar operation. However, we knew that at any moment the war could be back on again, this time with several of my fellow full-time commercial airline pilots right there on the front line. If we were shot down and survived but unable to make our way to friendly lines, we were prepared to accept our fates as prisoners of war. And, if necessary, we were all prepared to die for our country. We were prepared years before to make that ultimate sacrifice, which many of our close friends already had. They died not just in wartime. Most died in peacetime, the silent sacrifice not often publicized or recognized by civilian beneficiaries.

Fighter pilots are a special breed, but not so different from other warriors in that we are all prepared to die in battle from enemy fire, if it comes to that. We all volunteered and are willing to make that sacrifice. However, friendly fire is another story. To be wounded or killed by shots, like the anthrax vaccine, at the hands of our own country, the country that we serve, is a difficult pill to swallow.

We were not given anthrax shots for our first post-Gulf War deployment in 1997. Three years later though, facing our next deployment to the Gulf, we learned of this mysterious mandatory requirement to take the controversial anthrax shots. Why? That was the first question. What's different this time? Next question: Is the shot safe? And then: Why did eight part-time A-10 pilots in the Connecticut Air National Guard (CANG) refuse to take the shot?

These questions began my investigation of the fatally flawed anthrax shot policy. My life would change drastically; from here on, I would face monumental tests of courage and ethics. That famous quote from Thomas Paine hit home for me: "These are the times that try men's souls."[1]

Every war produces friendly-fire casualties. Conventional weapons and human judgment in wartime, plus the fog of war, combine to yield friendly-fire casualties, deaths caused by our own hands. Should we be surprised, then, that preparing for deadly biological warfare, developing offensive and defensive weapons for mass-destruction scenarios, would also do the same? This peacetime conflict, the AVIP controversy, in preparation for biological warfare is no different. Most friendly-fire casualties are the results of accidents, but the mandatory AVIP is different. It produces victims by intention.

Six deaths have been attributed to this program. Thousands have been injured. However, because this vaccination was never properly tested to meet the standards required by a sometimes vaccine-skeptic public, the losses are mounting. Victims who are unaware of the symptoms and their connection to the insufficient testing of the shots slowly and mysteriously watch their health deteriorate. The Defense Department denies any connection, but we would not expect it to admit responsibility and, therefore, liability. If the department follows its modus operandi, it will finally accept responsibility after enough people uncover the truth and after far too many people have died. Past behavior patterns suggest that the Defense Department may admit responsibility about fifty years from now, just as the Rockefeller Report has uncovered. In that document, the Defense Department was cited for serious ethical and medical violations, including the intentional exposure of military personnel to potentially dangerous substances, often in secret.[2]

Even if the evidence and the numbers were staggering, until public outcry demands reparations, supported by the media and the courts, victims will not receive relief, nor will the Defense Department end this program and make amends. Unfortunately, this process takes years. But these concerns about the AVIP and its casualties do not even include possible links of the anthrax shot with Gulf War illness, which would increase the victim list exponentially. Unfortunately, testing here is also inadequate.

No Gulf War Illness Testing

Note that the Defense Department denies any link between anthrax and Gulf War illness, just as it similarly denied the existence of Gulf War illness for at least five years. Of more than 130 studies funded by the Defense Department in the United States to explore the causes of Gulf War illness, none have looked specifically at the anthrax vaccine, although sixteen other causes have been studied. However, a single study on British veterans who received the British anthrax vaccine, a vaccine that is slightly different from ours, showed that the anthrax vaccine was highly correlated with Gulf War illness.[3] Until January 1999, already into our mandatory AVIP, there were no available published papers that considered any link between anthrax and Gulf War illness. Before that, several "expert" committees, lacking experience with anthrax, were asked to consider it. However, after influential Defense Department briefings, medical teams concluded that a relationship was unlikely. Then they specifically recommended against further research.

No Long-term Safety Testing

Besides Gulf War illness causal-link studies, most alarming is the fact that no long-term testing was accomplished on this vaccine. Kwai Chan, testifying for the GAO in an HGRC hearing on May 7, 1999, said that "these two vaccines, the original and the newly licensed one of the '70s [remember, it was licensed before the FDA existed], were made using different processes and have different data to support their safety. While these studies identified varying rates of adverse reactions, they did not question the safety of the vaccine." After forty-five years of using the vaccine on humans, we had hoped that his testimony would be different, saying that the vaccine's safety was tested before it was given on a mass scale.

Long-term testing is important in providing test subjects or volunteers some indication of what to expect from the shot. Long-term safety testing of the vaccine has not been accomplished. The costs of that faux pas alone, in terms of future victims with immune system deficiencies just waiting to be triggered because they've reached a vaccine saturation point, are anyone's guess. As the AVIP requires annual boosters, at what point in a twenty-year military career does the human body cry uncle?

On March 30, 2000, the National Academy of Sciences' Institute of Medicine, Committee on Health Effects Associated with Exposures during the Gulf War, concluded that "in the peer-reviewed literature there is inadequate/insufficient evidence to determine whether an association does or does not exist between anthrax vaccination and long-term adverse health outcomes."[4] Additionally, no carcinogenic testing was accomplished. Will it cause cancer? No one knows.

The Defense Department's Response: Four Studies

While the Defense Department points to four relatively short-term studies of adverse reactions to argue safety, Chan confirms that none of the studies questioned the safety of the vaccine itself. The studies may have reported on numbers, but that's different than testing for safety.

Here are results from the four studies that the Defense Department believes proves safety:

1. The CDC collected data for the IND study using an active/passive reporting system with just under 4,000 doses given. Local reaction rates were up to 30 percent, with up to 10 percent moderate/severe. These numbers are significantly higher than those reported on the vaccine product label. Is that considered safe?

2. In 1997, a Pittman study focused on 508 doses given, with fairly high local reactions of 21 percent (with 5 percent moderate or severe), plus high numbers of systemic reactions, 29 percent mild and another 14 percent moderate to severe with active monitoring.

3. The Tripler Army Medical Center in Honolulu conducted another active monitoring study of 536 doses in which local reactions were ignored, with a very high incidence (43 percent) of systemic mild reactions and 5 percent moderate to severe reactions. Such a high incidence of reactions is extremely significant when you consider the massive scale of this vaccination program. Systemic reaction rates of 20 percent were seen after just one of the first three injections. However, only four adverse-event forms from the passive reporting system used by the Defense Department were

filed, despite lost duty time and required medical attention. Also, in March 2000, we learned that the participants' vaccinations were terminated early, after only three of the required six doses were given. (The vaccine also requires annual boosters.) What was the criteria and explanation for this anomaly?

4. The fourth study is the ongoing vaccination program. The Defense Department claimed in testimony on March 16, 1999, that only forty-two reports on adverse effects were submitted to the FDA and the CDC for this program and that only seven service members required hospitalization or experienced loss of duty for more than twenty-four hours.[5] This ongoing study does not give us much long-term information.

Assuming that reports or studies of numbers are adequate to prove vaccine safety, as the Defense Department would have us believe, the numbers alone are quite unacceptable compared with other vaccines. The anthrax vaccine may be fifty times more likely to produce sick victims than established vaccines given to the public.

Safety Is Not a Numbers Game

A Korean study of 337 vaccinated service members shows reaction rates from minor to severe are 40 percent for men and 70 percent for women.[6] The reactions resulted in decreased work activity for 3 percent of males and 8 percent of females. A Fort Bragg study showed a 44 percent reaction rate. In April 29, 1999, congressional testimony, one Air National Guard squadron reported a 75 percent systemic rate of reactions from expired vaccine that was used. Many of the sick were too weak to work. Some took more than eight weeks to get diagnosis and treatment.

According to Dr. Renata Engler, chief of the allergy/immunology department at Walter Reed Hospital, the information on Dover Air Force Base attracted significant attention, because twenty to twenty-five service members reported Gulf War illness-like symptoms, resulting in a 50 percent reduction in function.[7]

These reaction rates are almost unbelievable for a mass immunization program of 2.4 million military troops. What's more, the Defense Department now admits, although still reluctantly, to fairly high reaction rates. The public would not tolerate a vaccine with these risks being made available to them without significant warnings. Pull the plug and end the experiment before the numbers get worse.

What's Wrong with Defense Department Numbers?

Poor record keeping has plagued the anthrax vaccine from the 1970 licensure for use with livestock workers, veterinarians, lab workers, and researchers at risk for infection. From 1974 to 1989, approximately 68,000 doses were distributed. However, the Defense Department cannot provide numbers of who and how many received the vaccine during this period. The GAO told Congress that between 200 and 2,000 were vaccinated, but no records were kept and no follow-up was done.[8] Numbers from other sources vary widely from 3,000 to tens of thousands.

In 1990, approximately 268,000 doses were distributed during the Gulf War. But only 170,000 or less were supposedly used on troops. Where are the rest? No one knows. Between 1991 and April 1999, 1.2 million were distributed.[9]

In 1996, the anthrax manufacturing facility became known as Michigan Biologics Products Institute (MBPI), an entity controlled by the state government of Michigan. In September 1998, a transfer of ownership changed the name to BioPort Corporation, the sole source provider and manufacturer of the anthrax vaccine. Until June 20, 2001, a total of 2,071,876 doses were given to 516,619 military, 74,000 of whom received all six shots.[10] There have been about 500 who have refused.[11] Adverse reactions numbering 1,578 have been reported, 208 of them classified as serious.[12]

On Oct 3, 2000, at an HGRC hearing, an epidemiologist warned the committee not to be swayed by emotion. "Let me implore you to look for risks in a quantitative fashion," said Alexander Walker, a professor at Harvard School of Public Health. "When it comes to making a decision about what will best protect the most people with the most efficient use of resources, the 6 million are more important than the one."[13]

No doubt, that nearsighted argument was used to say, "Don't worry about a few people who get sick or die in the military when you can protect the 2.4 million in the military with this exceptional vaccine!" Walker probably never considered the possibility that the vaccine could be a threat to 100 times that number, if the AVIP continued unchecked. With the immediate danger of this "quantitative fashion" perspective, perhaps we should be "swayed by emotion." Fear is an emotion that sometimes protects us from real danger.

But, sticking with Walker's plea to look for risks in a quantitative fashion, how about a common-sense numbers test using Defense Department numbers? At an October 20, 1995, meeting, a Defense Department slide showed a 1.3 percent systemic-reaction level from the vaccine. The department would have been horrified at the math if they did it—or maybe not. Based on 2.4 million troops, that would equal 31,200 troops with varying degrees of sickness. While that number provides job security for the military medical community, it fails the common-sense test. What capacity does the medical system have to handle such numbers?

But that's not all. On July 17, 1995—using the Defense Department's reaction-rate number once again—the rate was 1.77 percent. Notice that the Defense Department number was higher earlier in the year. (Maybe someone did the math and decided that the department had better revise the reaction rate downward, quickly, before the next briefing in three months.) Using the July number, the number of sick would be 42,480 troops.[14] How could the department handle that rate of illness? Perhaps that's why Defense Department numbers decreased in subsequent briefings. Those reaction-rate numbers applied to the public at large would have produced millions of sick and would have killed this program dead in the water, along with many of its victims.

Another thing the Defense Department doesn't tell you is how its passive reporting system is administered to benefit its own interests. Significant Vaccine Adverse Event Reporting System (VAERS) discrepancies were noted by the GAO in its investigation and in congressional testimony. So, even when the Defense Department studies tracked only reaction rates, it did a horrible job on that mission too.

Based on testimony from around the country, VAERS reports are sometimes not made for several reasons.

1. Many times clinics fail to make VAERS forms available to military members.
2. Those sick or injured are afraid to seek help or tell anyone for fear of jeopardizing their military careers.
3. They may also be afraid to admit symptoms to themselves and may be too uncertain to seek help.
4. Finally, if they report their symptoms and seek help, many times, based on nationwide accounts, their symptoms are minimized, then discounted as not associated with the shot.
5. The Defense Department, in most cases, discards VAERS forms that are filed, invalidating them for its own reasons in its own favor.

However, the Defense Department, in its ambitious efforts to inject its troops by 2005 without waking a sleeping public, uses this passive and poorly administered reporting/monitoring system to justify the safety of the program. Common sense tells us that using the basis of "reactions," also known as sick guinea pig tabulation, to test, then claim safety, is taking advantage of those human subjects. Use of this system suggests a desire to ignore safety tests or the need for them and to conveniently take advantage of a captive audience, like the "volunteer" military, to test the shot and gather numbers. The worst aspect is the fox-guarding-the-hen-house syndrome. The Defense Department pretends to be the advocate for the very people it is hurting, while it is immune from answering to either a civilian authority or the vaccine's victims.

What about the New Vaccine?

The new vaccine is significantly different from the original, so by all accounts, safety testing should have been done. The second, or modified vaccine, which is the one that the MDPH began using once the license was approved, differs from the original in three critical ways.

1. The manufacturing process was changed when the MDPH took over.
2. The strain of anthrax that Merck used to grow the original vaccine was changed, and another strain was used for the MDPH vaccine.
3. And finally, to increase the yield of the protective antigen, which is believed to be an important part of the vaccine's protective effect, the ingredients and recipe used to make the vaccine were changed from the original vaccine.[15]

The vaccine is made up of three parts: the protective antigen, edema factor, and lethal factor. Effective and safe vaccines necessarily keep these in proper balance. However, this anthrax vaccine is termed "undefined" by both civilian and military medical experts, and the ingredients vary from lot to lot, affecting their potency and safety.

We are haphazardly using a new vaccine that was never tested, a different vaccine from the one originally approved for use. Compounding this issue is the fact that changes were made in the manufacturing process in order to produce large quantities of the vaccine for the AVIP. Because of the significant legal implications, this issue is reviewed in more detail in chapter 6, but these modifications were significant enough to change the ugly "goo" in the syringe being injected into human bodies. The new goo may be up to a hundred times more potent. That is why, in congressional testimony, I emphatically stated, "We are the guinea pigs. We know it. And you know it."

How Much Did the Defense Department Know?

A 1985 Army Request for Proposal to solicit a new anthrax vaccine from the biological industry candidly discussed the safety and the efficacy of the Michigan vaccines—its high adverse-reaction rate and its questionable effectiveness against different strains of anthrax. From documents right out of Fort Detrick: "There is no vaccine in current use which will safely and effectively protect military personnel against exposure to this hazardous bacterial agent." "Highly reactogenic, [it] requires multiple boosters to maintain immunity and may not be protective against all strains of the anthrax bacillus."[16] These statements not only came from Defense Department officials, but they came from the same officials who, in a postconversion pro-anthrax setting, now claim the opposite. To troops, to the media, and in congressional testimony, Defense Department and BioPort officials, while acknowledging high reaction rates, continue to compare the anthrax vaccine's safety to influenza and other safe vaccines. But a recent study[17] shows that reaction rates to the anthrax vaccine may be as much as fifty times the combined rate of all vaccines given to the general public.

The resulting attitude seems to be one of putting safety on a lower shelf.

Safety aspects were low priority, since the vaccine had very limited distribution and limited circumstances under which this vaccine would be used. In limited vaccination programs, slighting safety may be appropriate. However, the vaccine's limited distribution and limited circumstances quickly changed when it was prescribed for 2.4 million of America's finest citizens.

How about a JVAP "cocktail"?

No "cocktail" tests were performed, which is the combined effects of receiving multiple vaccines that alter the immune system. What is the saturation point in the human immune system for multiple types of vaccinations? Is it different for everyone? What are the effects of reaching this saturation level? Considering anthrax alone, what is the maximum dosage over time? A twenty-year military career would require more than twenty shots of anthrax vaccine; how will that mix with other vaccines? How well can the human body handle the blitzkrieg of a dozen or more biowarfare vaccines? Nobody knows. The Defense Department doesn't. Neither does the National Institute of Health (NIH), nor the CDC, nor Fort Detrick, nor any other viable medical or scientific research organization.

This cocktail effect is vitally important because of the Joint Vaccination Acquisition Program (JVAP). The JVAP is a $322 million, ten-year program for the development, production, testing, FDA licensure, and storage of vaccines. A variety of sources estimate that a wide range (three to forty) of vaccines to protect U.S. armed forces against potential biological warfare agents are being developed.[18] According to military sources, there are more than sixty-five biological warfare agents and less than ten effective vaccines. Can the pace of development for effective vaccines match the ability of an aggressive nation to weaponize? No. Will the vaccines under the JVAP be subject to the same level of scrutiny and rigorous examination that the FDA applies to vaccine products for civilian use? Probably not. The cocktail effect is critical, because multiple vaccinations have already been reported to cause immune effects that result in symptoms similar to those of Gulf War illness.

Add, then, the probability that additional vaccines will also be untested by public standards. Will the test data be provided to civilian doctors? Or will the military withhold information and test results, as they did with the ingredients in the anthrax vaccine, and then place the program in the Defense Department spin cycle before releasing conclusions to the public? Once again, they would be preventing medical peer review and civilian scientific analysis of actual data and test results. We have allowed this process to go unchecked for too long.

Dr. Meryl Nass, a civilian and self-taught anthrax expert from Freeport, Maine, summarizes the concern: "As the JVAP moves forward, DOD [Department of Defense] will fund and control all steps in the vaccine process, from initial research and development to manufacturing and administering the vaccines.

If history is a guide, assessment of efficacy and safety, stringent manufacturing controls, and normal FDA oversight may be compromised. If the vaccines are licensed as proposed, no informed consent need be obtained and vaccinations will probably be mandatory. The Defense Department is assuming greater authority over the medical interventions given to troops at the same time that it has failed to follow agreed upon procedures for the use of experimental drugs and vaccines."[19]

Specifically, Nass suggested that we should expect more of the following: conflict of interest for those engaged in the process, insufficient testing of products or combinations, inadequate quality control of production-enforced administration of medical treatments or procedures that are not standard for civilians, inadequate record keeping, and lack of proper surveillance for side effects following use.

The cost of this program in terms of victims and dollars is probably more than we can imagine and certainly more than we can afford.

No Human Efficacy Testing

Efficacy simply means the ability of the vaccine to be effective and to produce the intended results. Chan's congressional testimony representing the GAO confirmed that no human efficacy testing of the vaccine was performed. Specifically addressing clinical trials using the original vaccine, Chan said "the only study of the efficacy of the vaccine for humans was performed by Philip S. Brachman during the 1950s. This, the only controlled field study, involved workers in four mills in the northeastern U.S. that processed animal hides. They routinely handled anthrax-infected animals."

Before vaccinations, the number of humans in these mills infected annually by anthrax was 1.2 per 100 employees. During the trial, twenty-six cases of anthrax infection were reported at the mills, five inhalation and twenty-one cutaneous. Four of the five who received inhalation anthrax died. No cases of inhalation anthrax occurred in vaccine recipients. Of the twenty-one cases of cutaneous anthrax, two individuals were partially immunized and one was fully immunized.[20] The vaccine was not capable of preventing infection in all cases.

Disputes occur on the Brachman numbers. Elsewhere in his text, he contradicts the number of anthrax cases. A 72 percent effective rate, not the 92 percent that Brachman claimed, may be more accurate, according to expert opinion. In any case, the number of individuals who contracted anthrax by inhalation was too low to assess the efficacy of the vaccine against this form, according to the Defense Department, the GAO, and expert testimony.

Given incidence rates before 2001, one must be suspicious about why 25 percent of all inhalation anthrax cases previously documented in the United States occurred in the four mills in the Brachman study and, coincidentally, during that efficacy trial. In the book *The River* by Edward Hooper (Little, Brown, 1999), there is speculation that a deliberate change in processing, which occurred on the first day of the Manchester, New Hampshire, epidemic, may have contributed to the field trial conditions for evaluation of the vaccine.[21] This change in the manufacturing process may have conveniently exposed workers so the test of the vaccine could be accomplished. The results show that under very limited test conditions, inhalation protection was provided in a small number of cases against a simple anthrax strain and that cutaneous protection was not complete, not a conclusive test for inhalation anthrax.

A February 1969 memorandum from a U.S. Department of Health, Education, and Welfare (HEW) committee concluded that, based on the data, the assumption of efficacy appeared speculative. Later, the FDA had its own uncertainties about the vaccine.

On December 13, 1985, the FDA *Product Review* concerning the anthrax vaccine stated that "efficacy against inhalation anthrax is not well documented." With its hands essentially tied by the Defense Department, the FDA was forced to blindly accept the numbers that the Defense Department provided for safety issues. On the same date, the *Federal Register* reported that "a final rule fully licensing the [anthrax] vaccine was not published" after requests by the NIH and the Public Health Service in previous decades for human efficacy data," and that "no meaningful assessment of its value against inhalation anthrax is possible due to its low incidence."[22]

In 1989, Assistant Secretary of Defense Robert B. Barker wrote to Senator John Glenn, "Current vaccines, particularly the anthrax vaccine, do not readily lend themselves to use in mass troop immunization for a variety of reasons: ... a higher than desirable rate of reactogenicity and in some cases lack of strong enough efficacy against infection by the aerosol route of exposure."[23]

Fortunately, the Defense Department's self-testing reached a point where it had overdrafted on the FDA's previously blank check. Throughout the 1990s, the FDA did not test lots itself but only reviewed results from the manufacturer and the Defense Department. A firm named Mitretek was hired to oversee the manufacturer's testing processes. Their review showed that of the thirty-one lots that were tested and that initially passed, twenty-five subsequently failed. Independent of Mitretek's review, the FDA also quarantined fourteen lots once it inspected the plant in 1998.

No Gender and Fertility Testing

Perhaps most offensive, females are documented to be victims of this vaccine at two to three times the male rate. Yet the AVIP continues. Additionally, no scientific fertility testing on females or males was ever accomplished.[24] The manufacturer admits that it is not known whether the anthrax vaccine is safe for pregnant women or for their offspring. So, America's young sons and daughters who are required to take this harmful shot do not know whether or not it will threaten their lifelong dreams of family.

Pregnancy tests may soon be required before getting anthrax shots because a Navy study made public in January 2002 suggests that vaccinations have resulted in birth defects. The study showing this higher incidence of birth defects is currently underway.

Testing Our Patience

No safety testing; no long-term tests; no Gulf War illness tests; no cocktail tests; no human efficacy tests, especially against inhalation anthrax; no carcinogenic tests; no gender testing; and no fertility tests—our patience should be tested. Testing this vaccine on humans, or friendly fire, is producing patients at a rate that is testing our patience limits. Friendly fire has become the major threat.

It is equally important to know where the real threat is coming from, so we should consider who is not shooting. Is an imaginary enemy creating our victims?

Anthrax in Warfare

In World War I, nerve gas and chemical warfare were prevalent. Nothing biological was used on a mass scale, although the war machines were experimenting with multiple weapon types. Germany reportedly used anthrax only against pack animals in World War I.

In World War II, during the 1930s, the Japanese studied anthrax and used it against China. Britain and the United States began studying anthrax in the 1940s. The British conducted experiments with anthrax bombs in 1942 on the island of Gruinard off the northwest coast of Scotland. Viable spores persisted there for more than forty years. The island was decontaminated in 1987 by soaking the soil with hundreds of thousands of liters of formaldehyde. Without decontamination, test data revealed that viable spores would have survived until at least 2050.

Another significant anthrax event involves its possible use in the civil war in Zimbabwe (Rhodesia) in 1979. The first documented large-scale use of anthrax occurred there, where it was used to kill cattle to deter their owners from harboring guerrillas. Nearly 200 deaths and 10,000 human cases of cutaneous anthrax were documented when the poor farmers ate meat from the dead animals. This story can be found in *Plague Wars* by Tom Mangold and Jeff Goldberg.[25]

Renaissance Island (translation from Russian Vozrozhdeniye Island), 850 miles east of Moscow, became a huge anthrax dumping ground following the warming of U.S.-Soviet ties in the spring of 1988. Even though this anthrax was bleached twice in sixty-six gallon containers, then dumped into sandy pits and buried for a decade under three to five feet of sand, some of the spores are still alive and potentially deadly. This is one of the characteristics that make anthrax such a desirable weapon. Anthrax is easy to store, easy to spread over a large area, and easy to produce in large quantities; it is highly lethal; and it is dangerous for a long time.

However, the point must be made that no country is now shooting at or threatening us with anthrax. Afraid of what might be in the shadows, we are shooting indiscriminately at imaginary and exaggerated targets. Intelligence confirms that there are no new biological threats (discussed further in chapter 3), except for us. We are the major threat. We are shooting our own with syringes of untested, unproven poison.

Fuzzy Medicine and Science

Like politicians and economists who use fuzzy math, anthrax vaccine proponents engage in both fuzzy science and fuzzy medicine. The JVAP may soon produce a laboratory filled with specimens, or victims of fuzzy science. We want to believe that both military and civilian doctors who have taken the Hippocratic oath have the same level of commitment to protect patients. The threat of medical malpractice would certainly prevent experimenting on civilians at this fuzzy level of medicine. Yet, in the hands of an ambitious military medical community and in the name of expediency and following orders, it seems, the ends are enough to justify any means. With accountability covered by a blanket of bureaucracy, there is virtually no threat of liability or accountability concerns for the military doctor who is pro-anthrax.

For example, when military officials testify under oath to Congress, they claim that the vaccine is effective against inhalation anthrax and against all strains of anthrax. Their conclusions have a shaky foundation in science, in fact, and in their own historical documents. Given that they may have desires and reasons to make such claims, their conclusions are even more suspicious and unacceptable at face value without investigation or further proof.

Beginning in the late 1980s, the Defense Department began studying the efficacy of vaccines on animals, using guinea pigs, rabbits, and monkeys. All of these studies support the view that in those animals, the licensed vaccine can protect against exposure to some strains of anthrax by either inoculation or inhalation. It is clear, however, that animal species differ in their susceptibility. Research using monkeys showed for the first time that monkeys could be protected against aerosol exposure. Especially good results with monkeys are achieved when the number of strains they are exposed to is limited, and great results are achieved if a strain is used that the Defense Department knows the vaccine is successful in defeating. The Defense Department is very good at designing studies to achieve the results in the laboratory that might already support its program, hardly a scientific method of experimentation or testing.

Plus, in both the guinea pig and monkey studies, protection did not correlate with levels of antibodies to a protective antigen. Thus, there is not adequate scientific explanation or medical understanding to justify an optimistic mind-set in comparing monkeys to humans. Several studies show no direct comparison of immunity in humans to that in monkeys. Study findings suggest that "the importance of various specified immune mechanisms against inhalation anthrax may vary in different animal species, or the ability of the licensed human vaccine to stimulate cell-mediated immunity may be greater in some species than others." A study as late as 1998 comes to the same conclusion and continues to emphasize the need for further studies.[26]

To base sweeping claims of safety and efficacy on inadequate scientific evidence promotes fuzzy medicine when that science is applied to humans in the form of a shot. But, the unknowns about anthrax do not stop there. They go from the fuzzy to the weird.

Weird Science, Weird Medicine

On January 7, 2002, the Associated Press reported that blood culled from military members who have been vaccinated against anthrax might be used to treat victims who were recently infected from the anthrax terror attacks. What testing was done on humans prior to the planning of these experiments? And is it adequate or even appropriate that these study results will be compared to monkey studies?

On the Fringes

Citizens who insist on safety, science, and objectivity must wonder about oversight of this program by the Defense Department when there is an inherent self-interest and conflict of interest. When it comes to citizens' and soldiers' rights, will the FDA, along with objective civilian scientists, be granted oversight, without being manipulated into being rubber stamps? This is a critical question now that postal workers and soon the public at large may be putting their trust in this program. Incredibly disturbing in current perspective is the fact that FDA access to this program was not allowed until 1993. Also disturbing is the military's ability to control access to information and to studies where there is no civilian peer review. The situation makes it easy to convince an entire nation and its free press that this vaccine is safe.

Inflation and exaggeration of the threat has propelled us far beyond reason and medical science. Inflation in the number of nations purported to have the capability and exaggeration in the capabilities they possess to make and use these weapons have created a straw enemy. Is it fear, bureaucracy out of control, or just plain insanity tolerated by an apathetic public and media? How did we get here?

"Who protects the force from ill-conceived force protection?" the HGRC asked.[27] Force protection is the new party line. While some have genuine motives and believe the claims of the AVIP, others feel forced to spew this party line up and down the military chain of command to help justify the program. The motive of career protection has cultivated an ostrich mentality of burying one's head in the sand until the dust settles, while praying that the shots will end with a cease-fire order. Indeed, the anthrax shot program must be considered "farce protection," a typical military knee-jerk reaction that many in the military are accustomed to. A similar strategy rules in the famous military solution to low morale: "all military leaves are canceled until morale improves." Likewise, the AVIP defies common sense. Congress recognizes the need to protect us from ourselves, but sadly, some military leaders have misplaced their protection priorities.

One could say that the Defense Department has regressed from force protection to false protection to farce protection.

For protection, in September 1998, Secretary of the Army Louis Caldera, on behalf of the Defense Department, granted indemnification to BioPort. This aimed to protect BioPort from legal liability for the AVIP. Also discovered on Secretary of the Army letterhead was a similar, earlier authorization from Secretary Togo West Jr. in 1992: "The obligation assumed by MBPI under this contract involves unusually hazardous risks associated with the potential for adverse reactions in some recipients and the possibility that the desired immunological effect will not be obtained by all recipients. There is no way to be certain that the pathogen used in tests measuring vaccine efficacy will be sufficient, similar to the pathogen that U.S. forces might encounter to confer immunity."[28]

West acknowledged questions regarding the effectiveness of the vaccine ten years ago. He said the anthrax program involved "unusually hazardous risks" because safety is also an issue. His words were good enough to cut MBPI some slack in liability for their product but not important enough to warrant investigation or protection for his own troops. Some would consider that a breach of command responsibility, authority, and at the very least, a breach of trust for the men and women soldiers that the Army secretary is supposed to represent.

Sanity a Victim

Not disclosing the potential dangers to our fellow citizens or demanding a higher standard and not providing information to our sons and daughters who are willing to sacrifice their lives for our safety and freedom allows this irresponsible behavior to continue unchecked. However, the volunteer military's willingness to sacrifice their lives was never meant to be taken so lightly. To die to keep liberty's hands free is noble. To die at the hands of a public who misuses or trivializes their lives and dreams to keep their own intact is a wretched abuse and a heinous criminal cause.

It must be pointed out that the shot victims—the dead and injured from the AVIP—are not wartime casualties. This is not a result of emergency actions for homeland security or abroad, but a combination of forces out of control, and it is unhealthy for our military force.

This program has produced casualties of peace, the cost of which we tolerate, to our own shame. The vaccine has not been sufficiently tested, but AVIP has certainly tested us. Where is the moral outrage? Where is our courage? History and principles of warfare have taught the military—unfortunately, in too many cases not very well—to know thine enemy. Well, we have met the enemy. And he is us.

CHAPTER 2

Ready ... Fire ... Aim!

Any nation that does not honor its heroes will not endure long.
                    —Abraham Lincoln

With malice toward none; with charity for all, with firmness in the right, as God gives us to see the right, let us strive on to finish the work we are in, to bind up the nation's wounds, to care for him who shall have borne the battle and his widow, and his orphan ... to do all which may achieve and cherish a just and lasting peace among ourselves.... Neither let us be slandered from our duty by false accusations against us, nor frightened from it by menaces of destruction to the government ... let us have faith that right makes might, and in that faith, let us, to the end, dare to do our duty as we understand it.
                    —Abraham Lincoln

An Unsafe Vaccine

I remember the day when this anthrax vaccine became real for us at Fort Wayne. Before I was selected to be the 163rd Fighter Squadron Commander, the ultimate role that every fighter pilot dreams of and strives for, I realized that I might soon be faced with some tough choices. Suddenly we found ourselves in a potentially controversial situation, trapped by the threat of a career-ending policy that made little sense.

We were standing by the operations desk, where the daily flying schedule was posted. This is the natural hangout for pilots hungry to fly and to get their adrenaline fix at 9 Gs (nine times the force of gravity) and 600 miles per hour. Young Captain Mike Stohler, nicknamed Stohli, asked if I had heard about the shot. I could see in his eyes a plea for guidance on this issue. Stohli knew there was a good likelihood that I would be in the hot seat as his commander soon, and this anthrax vaccine issue was just sizzling and waiting to christen me in the new job.

Typically, a fighter squadron commander is very close to his pilots, especially if he is a quality leader; he has direct operational control of the fighter pilots and, in this case, their F-16s. He is responsible for training his pilots to be mission-ready, to perform the mission successfully, and to return safely home to the spouse and kids. His pilots and technicians are his responsibility, in the air and on the ground, and he considers himself always to be on duty.

The fighter squadron commander has no room for errors; he is responsible for eighteen assigned F-16 fighters, valued at about $20 million each, and thirty to thirty-five pilots, in whom the Air Force has invested about $6 million each. We are trained to use excellent judgment in minimum-time scenarios, such as flying supersonic fighters at low altitude in rugged terrain and flying complex missions, single-seat, all alone. And we are expected to make even more outstanding decisions when time allows. Half a billion dollars in assets, not to mention the responsibility for lives at my command, made me careful not to take anything for granted, especially if it was important to the men. This vaccine policy would have to stand serious and severe scrutiny before I would take responsibility for injuring or killing any of my troops, either directly, by the shot itself, or indirectly, if a pilot's flying performance was impaired.

Stohli felt and endured the pain of personal sacrifice during this crazy process, as did many. He was one of our sharpest young pups. He was so good we sent him to Fighter Weapons School, the Air Force's Top Gun school. I tried to get Stohli and one of our other deserving pilots promoted after I became squadron commander, without success. Part of leadership's coercion and intimidation plan was to prevent promotions and attendance at schools for further training for members who did not agree to take the shot. It was premature for them to have to make a decision on the shot, which was nine months away, but leadership would not promote people who wouldn't commit early to taking the shot. This phenomenon was replicated around the country. While it is true that we expect more from people after they are promoted and given more responsibility, a promotion is also a reward earned for excellent performance. Stohli had earned the promotion and deserved it when I put him in for it. Many careers were negatively affected by the AVIP.

News of the eight A-10 pilots from the CANG who, in January 1999, drastically altered their careers by refusing to take the shot and resigning had become public and had filtered our way. Soon the rumors began about our facing the same dilemma, only it wasn't long before they weren't rumors anymore. Our wing commander, the officer in charge at our base, announced his intention to have us vaccinated in August 1999, a full nine months before our upcoming Middle East deployment. His motives for vaccinating so soon were unknown and barely understood but immediately threatening. We began researching, and during that process, I was selected as the 163rd Fighter Squadron Commander.

In our research, we soon discovered Dr. Meryl Nass, an internist who had written several articles about the shot's safety and effectiveness. Her specialized professional knowledge and medical objectivity were unmatched by our earlier research sources. Also, she had seen and treated serious anthrax reactions that included severe rashes, in which the skin peels off (Steven Johnson syndrome); endocrine organ failure, in which the testes, thyroid, and adrenal glands stop functioning; many different kinds of neurological reactions; many autoimmune, rheumatological diseases; chronic fatigue; and fibromyalgia. At her own expense and on her own time, she had investigated the possible use of anthrax in the 1979 civil war in Zimbabwe.

I contacted Nass by phone, and we met twice, as I intensified and she assisted in our research effort. I invited her to speak to my pilots at Fort Wayne. We made arrangements for her visit. Meanwhile, the documents and the disparity in facts between our research and the Defense Department's attempted snow job concerning the shot was unbelievable. I began to inform my boss, the wing commander, of the facts we were uncovering, some of which were blatantly contrary to the Defense Department's spin on the AVIP. Unimpressed by the contradictions and with no apparent curiosity for the truth, he said that our role was not to inform of the truth; we were supposed to only tell the Defense Department's version and to educate people using that information. He hedged when I asked him if he was suggesting that we censor information, especially when the truth could be harmful to the health of our troops.

What's more, the wing commander would not let Nass on base to speak to our pilots. So, we decided to have a pizza get-together downtown. The meeting lasted five hours, with twenty of our thirty-two pilots showing up. Needless to say, the issue had gotten their attention. About thirty enlisted personnel also came, as I thought it was important from a health and integrity standpoint that they also be informed. Many of these folks were crew chiefs and administrative personnel who worked shoulder-to-shoulder with pilots every day. Their challenges were even more severe. Many of them had commitments to the Air National Guard, so they couldn't simply resign like most pilots. Many were full-timers without the directly transferable job skills or career choices that pilots who could fly commercial airliners had. And some had many years invested, making it difficult for them to leave.

Nass showed slide after slide, with bibliographic references for further research and verification, while she pointed out the half-truths delivered by the Defense Department. She explored the data and test results that disproved their claims about the safety and effectiveness of the shot. Much of the contradictory information she shared came directly from the Army's own test data and included quotes from its own briefing slides and letters. Much of the information was retrieved using Freedom of Information Act requests, information that is available to the public upon request.

An interesting sidelight: our top flight surgeon at Fort Wayne, "Ben Arnold," a doctor, or more specifically, a psychologist, also attended our meeting. His spy mission was obvious to the pilots attending, but he was polite and asked a few questions. He did not participate in the discussion later; nor did he meet with pilots again for at least six months. He took plenty of notes and left early. Later, he participated in a typical Defense Department-style character assassination attempt, which the Defense Department commonly used as a tactic to attack those who did not support the AVIP. Before Nass could travel for a similar meeting with F-16 pilots in Madison, Wisconsin, negative information about her was relayed from the flight surgeon's office in Fort Wayne to prepare them for her visit. A civilian doctor who opposed the views of military medical officials was evidently considered a major threat.

I closed the meeting in order to hold a private session with the pilots for the last hour. After a short discussion, I asked how many would take the shots. Not one of the twenty pilots in attendance raised his hand. We then began to plan what steps we needed to take individually and as a group to protect ourselves. Also visiting Fort Wayne with Nass were three enlisted full-time Guard personnel from Battle Creek, Michigan, who were sick from the shot. They were Robin Groll, Randi Allaire, and David Churchill, all of whom testified at congressional hearings. I met with them for lunch. Playing devil's advocate, I grilled them from a very skeptical viewpoint, trying to believe in and support the shot program and have them convince me otherwise.

The stories of their treatment and symptoms were shocking. Not only were they sick, but they also suffered ridicule, disrespect, and lack of adequate medical care. I informed the wing commander later that same day that most of his pilots had said that they would not take the shot. He was angry, questioned our pilots' commitment level and loyalty, and continued to defend the AVIP. I defended our pilots' commitment level and offered examples of our fellow pilots who were war veterans but who would not be "shot" by our own country and become victims of our insanity. I explained that their loyalty is not to a controversial program but rightly focused on serving their nation. When their nation turns its back and does not support their basic human rights and constitutional rights, they may have to defend themselves and their families' future security to ensure their own protection.

I also tried again to ensure that our part-time Guard pilots would receive proper medical treatment if they became ill from the shot, knowing that even the three full-timers from Battle Creek who became sick were neglected. The promises offered were empty and based on general support, nothing specific. No guarantees would be provided in writing, because the Defense Department could deny that symptoms were caused by the shot.

Years of resentment and jealousy toward part-timers seemed to boil inside our wing commander, who spent years as a full-timer. He often spent long hours supporting and doing paperwork for airline pilots who would visit Fort Wayne at their convenience, fly their fighters, and go home to their other jobs. Emotion ruled when objectivity and reason should have, especially on safety issues that affected our pilots in the cockpit.

For pilots who aren't legally allowed to self-medicate with anything stronger than aspirin, whether it's military or commercial airline flying, safety in a single-seat aircraft is always paramount. The symptoms I saw before my very eyes from our Battle Creek visitors, plus the reports that Nass was receiving from the field, were extremely disturbing and a threat to flying safety. She was getting much more information about people who were sick from the shot than the Defense Department was from its shoddy VAERS program because, as a civilian doctor, she could be trusted to treat them seriously for the proper cause of illness and with a potential cure that denial never would. These concerns were valid and convincing and demanded appropriate responses.

The symptoms—dizziness, blackouts, fatigue, and blurred vision—would concern any F-16 squadron or wing commander, even if hardware and bent metal were all he cared about. Safety and protecting resources, even in combat, are always the highest of priorities.

Armed with facts from extensive research, I developed a briefing outline that discussed the lack of safety, effectiveness, and ethics in this program, and I shared it with the wing commander. Although he had never said as much, others around the base who evidently had less to lose from serious illness had accused pilots who refused to take the shot of being wimps, afraid of a silly shot. But civilians and probably 95 percent of the military have no clue of the incredible professionalism, dedication, determination, patriotism, intelligence, commitment, and camaraderie of fighter pilots. I was privileged to lead and work with an elite group. I explained to my boss why these highly trained, motivated, loyal, highly educated, and intelligent pilots and leaders would not subject themselves to an experiment or make, in his eyes, "a stupid choice." The fact is I didn't see much of his eyes, because he stared at the ceiling during most of my briefing, which unfortunately fell on intentionally deaf ears.

I could not run from the responsibility that I felt for my troops, who needed an advocate. In addition, those on active duty were being forced to take a shot that they probably knew little about, compared with what we had learned in a short time. If they knew even part of what we knew, and refused the shot, they were being court-martialed. I decided I would travel to Washington, D.C., as a civilian, a citizen-soldier, and I would try to gain as much support as I could to stop this unsafe, unethical, unlawful, and ineffective shot program.

Instead of fighting for safety, we were now playing a game of politics, policy, and power. My new name was David, and the enemy was Goliath. I knew I was proactively making a decision to become a participant rather than an unsuspecting pawn or spectator in that game. At the time, I could not imagine a scenario where the public would face the same choice. Now, we can all see how quickly many civilians could be facing that same choice. By taking a stand, even if for no other reason now than that the vaccine was unsafe, I knew that other shots would be fired at me too, just as they had been fired at others who opposed the AVIP. But I was ready.

Force Protection?

" Ready ... Aim ... Fire" has traditionally been a better sequence than "Ready ... Fire ... Aim." The AVIP used the latter form, firing before aiming properly. They fired with six shots per person in the first eighteen months and with annual booster shots to follow. It could be argued that the Defense Department was not ready to use this untested vaccine as a defensive weapon. But the Defense Department thought it was, and thinking it was ready caused the next problem. The Defense Department's aim was force protection. The parameters that should have surrounded and guided a solution to this goal were not recognized. Their aim of force protection was obscured by "target fixation."

Target fixating is a term that fighter pilots use to help develop a disciplined mind-set to avoid crashing when dive-bombing a target. While trying to sort through the myriad items located in a target area in an extremely short period of time—pointing at the ground and traveling at very high speeds—and trying to specifically identify and attack only the target, discipline must be maintained. Sometimes, unintended targets can be dangerous distractions. Unintended targets, or "friendlies," are often too close to the battle lines, and they can get hurt or killed when mistakes are made.

Overfocusing on the target is another subtle danger. Target fixation can cause even experienced fighter pilots to get sucked in, not realizing the serious dangers that are nearby. An air of invulnerability can quickly lead to an error of unrepairability. With time compression, the heat of the battle, and with an intense desire to succeed, many fighter pilots have hit the ground, not noticing normal safety cues that they should have recognized in time to break off the bombing pass at the target. The Defense Department has become target fixated, has not addressed the real dangers of the AVIP, and has not aborted the pass. A dangerous situation is still at hand.

At the beginning, the Defense Department's intended target, its aim of force protection, was not clearly isolated from the hidden dangers. The next chapter will review in greater detail the perceived threat that drove this AVIP solution. However, the Defense Department was unable to step back and see the greater picture. The Pentagon did not maintain the discipline needed to prepare a defensive weapon safe or effective enough to accomplish the objective. Unintended targets were hit. Force protection that accidentally injures friendlies is not force protection at all. The Defense Department pulled the trigger too soon; it fired at a worst-case, exaggerated, and probably relatively nonexistent threat. And as the proverb goes: He who aims at nothing is bound to hit it.

The Defense Department shot the proverbial arrow into the air, and where it landed, the department thought or hoped no one would care, or at least not enough to do something about it. The result of "Semi-ready ... Fire ... Aim" was a huge "Oops." The reality is no joke, as you will soon understand.

In the last chapter, we saw examples of how we victimized unintended targets or guinea pigs by lack of testing. We will now describe the results and costly casualties in further detail.

Death Not a Deterrent to Truth

BioPort's controversial vaccine may have contributed to the death of one of its own 220 employees on July 7, 2000. Richard Dunn, 61, who had cared for and monitored test animals at BioPort since 1992, received eleven doses of the vaccine over eight years, the last in April, and was dead by July that same year. One month after his shot, he complained of fatigue and swelling. Company doctors disavowed any connection to the vaccine, a common tactic that the Defense Department had used before with numerous victims. (Half the employees at BioPort have taken the six-dose regime.) The autopsy, according to Dr. Robert Joyce of the Ionia County Chief Medical Examiner's Office, showed an inflammatory response throughout Dunn's body. Dunn was found to have died from a heart attack after polyarteritis nodosa, an autoimmune disease in which the body mistakenly attacks its own arteries. However, the death certificate remains "politically correct" from the Defense Department's standpoint, listing the immediate cause of death as ventricular arrhythmia, allowing wiggle room for the Defense Department and BioPort to deny connection claims to the shot. Even though no signs of the deadly bacteria were found in his body, after speaking with Mrs. Dunn, I'm convinced that his body's reaction to the vaccine contributed to his death.

Of the six who died within a short time of getting the vaccine, three had cardiovascular problems, one committed suicide, one had cancer, and one died of a rare blood disorder. Lieutenant Colonel Dr. John Grabenstein, an epidemiologist who tracks reactions to the vaccine, said adverse side effects are minimal. Describing how a panel of civilian experts have looked at the deaths and found no evidence that they were caused by the vaccine, he offered a condescending explanation: "People are saying, 'I'm sick and I've been vaccinated.' I'm sorry that you're sick."[1] He continued by saying that A following B doesn't mean that B caused A. A civilian-expert panel called the Anthrax Vaccine Expert Committee has been established to determine such links between symptoms and shots. Presumably, if they haven't ruled on a case yet, we can't know if there is a link to the vaccine.

Those Dying at Dover

Like those who died, several pilots at Dover Air Force Base experienced dangerous symptoms from the shot. On May 5, 1999, the wing commander at Dover, Colonel Felix Grieder, made a stunning announcement. When legitimate questions about sicknesses at his base from the shot were not answered to his satisfaction, he called a safety "time-out" and ordered a temporary ceasefire on shots for his 3,600 service members. Several people at Dover were exhibiting symptoms similar to Gulf War illness (GWI). Twelve hours after his third shot, one pilot began showing side effects that limited his abilities and that eventually resulted in his being grounded and having his driver's license revoked. His symptoms included dizziness, rash, ringing in the ears, blackouts and moderate memory loss, uncontrollable shaking, and a near-final diagnosis of lupus. Reports like this made me thankful for my decision to try to protect my troops and strengthened my resolve.

Air Force Captain Michelle Piel, a pilot from Dover, required eight months and twelve doctors to find any reason for her symptoms of fatigue, dizziness, joint pain, coldlike symptoms, and immune disorders. She was grounded from flying, losing her hard-earned flight status. She was too sick to fly and too sick to take another shot. She became uncharacteristically ill after taking her first two anthrax shots. However, because her symptoms did not fall within expected parameters for vaccine reactions, doctors at Dover discouraged and dissuaded her from filling out a VAERS form. They would not associate her symptoms with the shot. It took her six months to reach the correct highly specialized doctors to begin to diagnose her immune system problems and help her find a solution.

Four other people came forward with symptoms. Several others were afraid to come forward for fear of being grounded. Ridicule came from the Air Force's flight surgeon teams, who gave inadequate and demeaning responses at briefings. Responses like, "It may be your time to get sick," or "These symptoms occur with other vaccinations as well," and, most disturbing, "I don't know, I don't care" were the standard responses from around the country. Coercion became a standard tactic as well. By FDA standards, reactions to the shot should have been treated and the immunizations discontinued. Only in a small number of cases did the Defense Department comply with this directive. The department denied symptoms and connections to the shot and expected service members to take the next shot.

Captain Bill Law, also a pilot at Dover Air Force Base, noticed a cyst after his fourth shot. This was diagnosed as a rare bacterial infection. Doctors said that if he had not checked into the hospital, he would have died. Now, even though his health is improving, he is grounded from flying, because the infection could come back at any time.

Because of his actions, Grieder was summoned from Dover to Washington for a counseling session. The result was that Grieder's wing commander position was promptly taken away and he was reassigned. Simultaneously the Air Force surgeon general, Lieutenant General Charles Roadman, came to the base to deliver the Defense Department "official answers" about the vaccine to the troops.

Others Sick

In Battle Creek, Michigan, nine of twelve personnel from a small unit preparing to deploy to the Middle East were given the shot and became sick. Three of those were seriously ill. They were harassed and the officers made an example of them. They were called malcontents and poor workers, even though they had excellent work records. Worse, they could not get the medical treatment that they needed and deserved. Their symptoms were similar but very troubling for any fighter pilot and included memory loss, chills, fatigue, muscle aches, and dizziness.

I spoke with my pilots, sharing my concerns about the health, safety, and liability aspects of the vaccine. However, I was careful to articulate and emphasize that it was a matter of individual choice and that they should make an informed decision. My goal was to provide all the information I could so that they could make the right decisions for themselves. I did not want to use my command position to unduly influence their choice either way.

For an F-16 fighter squadron, safety is always a primary consideration and is critical for determining any course of action, so the safety aspect of the shot was enough to get anyone's attention. But equally disturbing was that these full-time Guard troops from Battle Creek could not get the necessary medical attention.

Plus, the military was denying the existence of their symptoms and any connection to the shot. If the Defense Department accepted no responsibility or liability for its own full-time employees, serious doubts existed about the health care that would be extended to part-time pilots, who make up as much as two-thirds of a Guard fighter squadron.

At Fort Wayne, the shot program produced more than a handful of sick people whom I personally know, many secretly sick. To protect their job statuses, they keep their "sick" secrets from Guard officials. They realize that they won't get medical help and that they might lose their status as "deployable," which then damages or essentially ends their careers. For example, one of our F-16 crew chiefs got sick from the shot. He kept a diary and sought medical help elsewhere but waited two months before telling the doctors on base what was going on. Of course, the medical folks minimized his symptoms and suggested that it was mostly in his head.

At one of the nine hearings conducted by the HGRC, the GAO described another incident that occurred when it was on the road visiting bases and pilots who were faced with the shot dilemma. A pilot reportedly came after hours, quietly and secretly, when he wouldn't be seen by anyone, and showed officials the extremely limited movement in his abnormally shaped hand that he said was caused by the anthrax shot.

Countless people touched by this vaccination program know of fellow troops and friends who are secretly sick and who, in some cases, are receiving secret medical care on their own from civilian doctors.

The Sick and Their Symptoms

The early symptoms described from the anthrax vaccine include headaches, malaise, respiratory distress, chills, diarrhea (sometimes bloody), fever, and abdominal cramping. Symptoms often worsen after the third or fourth shot. Later chronic symptoms include dizziness, chronic fatigue, chest pains, sleep disorders, memory loss, headaches, joint and muscle pain, peripheral sensory neuropathies, intermittent diarrhea and abdominal pain, and recurring rashes. Other known symptoms from the anthrax vaccine include blackouts, autoimmune diseases, swelling of the limbs, nausea, night sweats, muscle and joint pain, ringing in the ears, cysts, tunnel vision, seizures, and fatigue. Nearly fifty different reactions have been reported from the shot. Most of these could pose an immediate physiological threat to a military fighter pilot in the cockpit.

Within six weeks of his fifth shot, Master Sergeant Clarence McNamer of Vacaville, California, experienced severe symptoms. He wrote to the *Air Force Times*. "I began to experience severe insomnia, headaches, twitches in my right arm, involuntary tremors and complete loss of scalp hair, eyebrows, and facial hair ... eyesight worsened, hot and cold flashes, exhausted all the time, chest pains, shortness of breath and moments of memory loss, feel and look like I've aged 20 years. Some of the symptoms have subsided but I am concerned about the long-term effects," he said.[2] With most people, the vaccine has its worst effects after the third or fourth shots.

Laurie spoke to reporters for her father, Air Force Reservist Earl Stover, because his symptoms are so severe and limiting. He has health problems every day from ringing ears to chronic fatigue to memory loss. Previously a very strong man who hung drywall, he can barely walk or keep his balance.

Jason Nietupski, an Army reservist, was diagnosed with an autoimmune disorder caused by the first shot and became markedly worse after the next two. His symptoms ranged from sores all over his mouth to blood clots in his legs, which make him unable to stand for long periods. Not only does he suffer from chronic fatigue syndrome but he has been diagnosed with an allergic reaction called Stephen Johnson syndrome. His medical records are six to eight inches thick, from his own description.

Thomas J. Colisimo of Pennsylvania, once an amateur weightlifting competitor, now gets winded pulling his wheelchair out of his pickup truck. He had the typical, fairly serious symptoms from the first two shots. The third resulted in nine cysts on his scalp that had to be surgically removed, one the size of a half-dollar. Still, he didn't associate these symptoms with the shot until his fourth one in September 1999. From this, he lost fifty pounds and began unexpectedly passing out. Three months later, he was suffering from fatigue, tunnel vision, and the first of his blackouts, which lasted thirty to forty-five minutes. He suffers from low blood pressure, memory loss, depression, explosive and unexpected loss of bowel control, and cognitive difficulties. Sleep apnea causes him to stop breathing in his sleep up to sixty times per hour.

Military doctors told him that the cysts were probably from a milk allergy, that everything else was psychosomatic, and that he was starving himself. They would not allow him to see his own medical records, saying they were confidential. He was told that his symptoms were not anthrax-related and that he had to take the fifth shot, which he refused. He was admitted to Walter Reed Army Medical Center in Washington, D.C., but only after congressional involvement got him the medical attention he needed and deserved. He was diagnosed with "anthrax intoxication" caused by the shot, according to hospital records.

While current claims and literature from the Defense Department say that the vaccine is a dead virus, after seeing Jason's and Tom's conditions in person, I have to conclude that the Defense Department really does not know the precise content of the vaccine. In a vaccine textbook by Dr. Philip Brachman and Colonel Arthur Friedlander, M.D., chief of bacteriology at Fort Detrick, the authors are vague about the protective antigen (PA): "No direct determination of the content or structure of the protective antigen in the vaccine have been made, and it is unknown whether the protective antigen is biologically active."[3]

Rates

Local reactions are mild in 30 percent of vaccine recipients. The inflammation usually occurs within twenty-four hours and subsides by forty-eight hours. The reaction area may grow to three to five centimeters in diameter at the injection site. These tend to increase in severity by the fifth injection, then may decrease in severity with subsequent doses. Subcutaneous nodules may occur at the injection site and persist for several weeks in a few persons. More severe local reactions are less frequent and consist of extensive edema of the forearm in addition to the local inflammatory reaction.

Systemic reactions to the shot are anything more severe than a local reaction in the vicinity of the vaccination. The product label says 0.2 percent of recipients experience malaise and lassitude. Unpublished trials at Fort Detrick, however, showed systemic reaction rates of 20 to 48 percent when active surveillance was employed, according to Nass in her April 29, 1999, congressional testimony.[4]

However, a U.S. Army Medical Research Institute of Infectious Diseases (USAMRIID) briefing slide for 1998 reported, "Reactogenicity rates for Systemic reactions: 0.7-1.3 percent."[5] Even if the military understated that number in its favor, that would leave us with 31,200 sick with systemic reactions and 93,600 severe local reactions, if we vaccinated all 2.4 million troops. If this were a civilian vaccine, those astronomical numbers certainly would not meet the standard of public trust, let alone FDA approval. The same briefing slide further acknowledged that the anthrax vaccine components are completely undefined in terms of characterization and quantification of the PA, other bacterial products, and constituents present. Also, there is significant variation in PA content from lot to lot.

Besides the problems that could be anticipated from the vaccine itself, the Defense Department also knew of the legal hurdles of informed consent. The department anticipated having enough volunteers for the shot program and knew that access to the subjects of the experiment and the monitoring of results would be difficult unless the department made it a mandatory military medical experiment. Chapter 6 contains further discussion of the legal ramifications of the shot program.

VAERS Discrepancies

The BioPort vaccine insert now warns that up to 34 percent of recipients will suffer mild reactions. But a GAO study in the year 2000 claimed actual local-reaction rates of 76.2 percent and systemic rates of 23.8 percent. As one would expect from the Defense Department's history of integrity problems in this program, the VAERS reports offer much lower numbers than the actual GAO numbers from the field.

When the GAO visits sites, its surveys are anonymous, convincing people that they can answer honestly, without fear of repercussions. Some physicians fear VAERS forms philosophically, because they have taken an oath to "first do no harm," and they worry that they may be reported for giving a harmful vaccine. In most cases, VAERS forms were not made available to military personnel, for whatever reasons. A former FDA director says only 10 percent of reactions are ever reported. The 1970s swine flu vaccine analysis shows that the military reports at only one-seventh of that 10 percent rate. Attorney Mark Zaid, who has defended several court-martial cases concerning the AVIP, claimed that the adverse-reaction rate is 175 times the rate that the Pentagon is reporting.[6]

According to Nass, the rates alone, up to 200 times those expected, based on the package insert, should have triggered an investigation and recall. She said, "There is not a single published study of the efficacy or safety of the current vaccine in humans."[7] This lack of safety is evidenced by the number of victims and their symptoms.

The FDA reported a dramatic increase, from 42 adverse reactions by March 1999 for 643,000 shots, to 1,561 by October 2000 for nearly 2 million shots given to 500,000 service members. Another thorn in the side of the Defense Department, Major Russ Dingle, said: "Put in context, this tripling of vaccinations caused an almost fortyfold increase in reported adverse reactions. These adverse reaction rates are almost fifty times the annual VAERS rate when compared to all vaccines administered to the population at large."[8] That provides a good comparison of the safety performance of anthrax to the safety performances of other vaccines.

VAERS reports typically provide some very low numbers. VAERS tracking began in 1990, and through April 1, 1999, only 101 reports of adverse events were reported associated with the anthrax vaccine. Of those, eighty-seven were nonserious injection-site edema (swelling with fluid in the tissue), injection site hypersensitivity, rash, headaches, and fever. Most of the fourteen individuals who suffered serious reactions have recovered. Three patients were hospitalized for injection site reactions. One experienced a more widespread allergic reaction. One was hospitalized with a confirmed case of aseptic meningitis nine days after vaccination. Another individual experienced Guillain-Barré syndrome within twenty-four hours of the third dose. He was unable to walk for nine days. He gradually recovered and his symptoms resolved within five months of the vaccination. Three weeks after receiving the vaccine, another individual experienced bipolar disorder and has not recovered.[9]

Unproven Force Protection, the report from the HGRC, states that the "safety of the vaccine is not being adequately monitored. The program is predisposed to ignore or understate potential safety problems due to a passive adverse-event surveillance system (VAERS) and Defense Department institutional resistance to associating health effects with the vaccine."[10]

The Defense Department's Easy Out

The Defense Department and anyone testifying or speaking on its behalf is quick to point out and to emphasize numerous times that reactions do not necessarily mean "causal" links. The department belittles its own sick personnel by saying that "more shots are being given, so expect more reactions" and "some of those people were going to get sick anyway." In other more direct words, we should accept the fact that it was just their time to get sick. These are wonderful, comforting words to hear from a commander who forced you to take an unsafe and untested shot. With the VAERS already known for underreporting, an institutional culture hostile to ill-health reports and intent on executing the AVIP only compounds the lack of accurate reporting.

Defense Department doctors at Dover Air Force Base explained that the symptoms are "psychological" and suggested "putting them on Prozac" and telling the victims "they are slackers and malingerers." Because they were so easily dismissed and certain that their illnesses were not getting reported by VAERS or doctor visits or up the chain of command, personnel at Dover began doing their own survey. Here are the results:

Of the 252 surveys that were sent, 139 were completed and returned (55 percent), 11 were returned by the postmaster, 4 with known illnesses did not respond, and 2 had not begun the vaccinations. Of the four with known illnesses, one had tuberculosis with skin lesions, one had chronic fatigue syndrome with chronic bone and joint pain, one had recurring seizures and one had Guillain-Barré syndrome and was paralyzed from the neck down.

Of the 139 respondents, 81 had probable systemic reactions (58 percent). These included 57 with joint or muscle pain or both, 41 with loss of energy or fatigue, 36 with reduced concentration, 34 with short-term memory loss, and 24 with difficulty sleeping.[11] Only 41 sought flight surgeon treatment, and only 17 filled out VAERS forms.

In bullet phrases from the grass roots of only one squadron, we get a sense of the "safety" the Defense Department touts for this vaccine. Comments on their symptoms include thyroid damage; autoimmune disorder; chronic fatigue; dizziness; grounded for several months; cysts inside and outside the body, including the heart; hooked up to an IV for six weeks after surgery to remove cysts; incapacitated at the controls of the aircraft due to illness; rash over most of the body; chronic joint pain; arms in braces from severe joint pain; crippling bone and joint pain; ringing in the ears; memory lapses; twenty-seven new allergies for one person; battling various infections; eight seizures for one individual; loss of ability to concentrate; lesions on pelvis, skin, and ribs; throat lesions; spots on the lungs; five incapacitating vertigo episodes for one person; hooked up to ventilator; paralyzed.[12]

With the Defense Department in denial, there is not much help for those who are sick. Defense Department doctors, unable to act as advocates for individual patients in the face of command pressure to meet force inoculation goals, have not defended or protected their own troops. Imagine being that squadron commander. Would you feel better knowing that you could hide behind a program and say you were just following orders? Would you feel justified if only 24 percent of your squadron, if you were lucky, didn't get sick? Would you still feel justified in saying it's a safe shot if you were in the unlucky bunch and 80 percent of your squadron had unacceptable reactions? Would you feel any better prepared for a hypothetical battlefield after taking the shot? Or would you think that it would only increase the odds that the enemy would try to biologically defeat the protection, requiring more shots and further risks? Does it matter that you feel justified legally and ethically, when the reality staring you in the face is sick coworkers and ex-friends?

As I queried members of Congress in my testimony, "Which symptom would you choose as an F-16 pilot? Which one would you choose to force on someone else, one of your friends or troops under your command?"

As Dover illustrates, the Institute of Medicine properly questions the value of the VAERS as limited in its usefulness for assessing the rate or causality of adverse events, as the information may be underreported, incomplete, or duplicative and may not always have been confirmed by medical personnel. The institute further states that no long-term follow-up was accomplished. And the famous Brachman trials made no attempt to study either local or systemic reactions after forty-eight hours following each shot. But now, the institute strongly encourages the development of active monitoring studies that evaluate long-term safety in recipients of the anthrax vaccine.[13]

Cause Tracing of Gulf War Illness

Cause tracing and denial are at the core of the safety issue, and research has not resolved it. Before the 1991 Gulf War and before he had his anthrax "conversion" experience and became a proponent of the AVIP, General Ronald Blanck (later the Army surgeon general) described the lack of published data regarding serious safety issues. But there were other problems in the Gulf War besides lack of safety information or lack of testing and research on the anthrax shot.

Vaccine arrived at military clinics without labels specifying the name of the vaccine product (presumably, to keep military secrets) and without package inserts. The bottles were labeled with lot numbers only. The question is, did they leave MDPH (now BioPort) like this, and could they have been relabeled or otherwise altered before they arrived in the Gulf, for example? Much of the evidence was destroyed on location. Everything connected with the shots was destroyed, burned up in fifty-five-gallon drums—all the packaging and empty vials.

To further complicate matters, in most cases, records were not kept on who received shots from specific lot numbers. Troops did not have immunizations recorded in their shot records. They were deliberately omitted from their permanent medical records, even when service members requested that they be specifically noted. Evidently the Defense Department tracks immunizations of their service dogs better than the shot records of their own troops.

Now, declassified documents identify the mysterious "Vaccine A" (seen as Vac-A, VacA-1, or VacA-2) as anthrax in only a limited number of shot records. The Defense Department has been unable to supply an alarming number of medical records for studies concerning the exposure of Gulf War veterans. There has been no accountability from our military medical personnel in the Gulf War, a familiar pattern with the AVIP.

Later in February 1994 (Senate Report 103-97), then Major General Blanck acknowledged a possible link between GWI and the anthrax vaccine: "It was rarely used [prior to the war]. Therefore, its safety, particularly when given to thousands of soldiers in conjunction with other vaccines, is not well established. Anthrax vaccine should continue to be considered as a potential cause for undiagnosed illness in Persian Gulf military personnel."[14] Blanck later disavowed his testimony when the AVIP was implemented. A drastic career-enhancing conversion must have taken place. Congressman Burton was among the legislators who described this new attitude as "evasive" in March 2000. Blanck's comment in the *Washington Times* was, "All panels ... have concluded that there is no evidence of a connection between the illnesses and any of the vaccines, either singly or in combination."[15]

After ten years, squandering more than $300 million and 193 studies (with 116 completed) as of January 24, 2002, the Defense Department and the Veterans Administration (VA) are essentially saying that they're not sure there is such a thing as GWI. The Defense Department hides behind statements like the one offered by Dr. John Feussner, "Several large epidemiological studies have shown that Gulf War [GW] veterans do not suffer from a unique, previously unrecognized GW syndrome." He quotes conclusions from an IOM report published in 2000, "Thus far, there is insufficient evidence to classify veterans' symptoms as a new syndrome."

In a March 2, 2001, letter to Dr. Kwai Chan of the GAO, Dale Vesser, acting special assistant to the secretary of defense for GWI, stated, "Finally, we note that similar poorly explained symptoms have been observed among veterans after all major wars in the last 130 years and that the British, Australians, Canadians, and Americans have found similar symptoms among GW veterans despite different exposures. These observations argue strongly that health problems among GW veterans are the result of multiple factors that are not unique to the Gulf War." Excuses like that have perpetuated the lack of accountability that our veterans must constantly face.

The new administration may change that trend. As President George W. Bush stated, "All that is going to end. In the military, when you are called to account for a mistake, you are expected to give one simple answer: 'No excuse, sir.'"

With the private sector providing promising research and scientific evidence, it is time to cut off funding to a bureaucracy that perpetuates incompetence at taxpayer expense. For example, one of the lessons learned after spending these hundreds of millions of dollars is something that has probably been known to medical doctors for hundreds of years. Feussner described this lesson in congressional testimony January 24, 2002. He responded with an explanation of how we must listen to our patients (veterans) when they are sick and of how, when they tell us they are sick we have to listen to them. Wow! Now that's results. After ten years and more than $300 million, we should be outraged. The truth is that our sick veterans have been questioned, criticized, scrutinized, and dismissed without proper care too often.

For example, too much money has been spent on internal studies and reviews of scientific literature, like money awarded to the Rand Corporation for this purpose. It does little to further science but it does make some Rand analysts a little smarter. And it results in very little, if any, benefit to veterans.

Most Americans rejoiced in the low number of casualties from our Gulf War success. However, wounds from the modern battlefield are not as obvious as they were in previous wars. As of March 1, 2001, out of the 700,000 military deployed, 504,047 are veterans, separated from service and eligible for veterans' benefits. An incredible total of 263,000 sought medical care at the VA, 185,780 (36 percent) have filed claims. From the 171,878 claims processed, 149,094 (80 percent) were approved in part from a war that lasted just over four days. Comparatively, Vietnam had 9.6 percent, Korea 5 percent, and WWII 6.6 percent qualify for disability benefits. More than 9,600 Gulf War veterans have died.

However, there remains a culture of denial, where the Defense Department and the VA ignore and deny scientific clues. This denial seems obvious when one is made aware of the fact that more than 14,000 chemical-agent detection devices sounded repeatedly during the war but they were all discounted as false alarms. Millions have been spent on public relations, although the Defense Department and the VA essentially admit that they have no answers for the causes of GWI. Consensus from the "PR machine" labels stress as the major cause. Most researchers, however, doubt that stress is a major cause. Psychiatrists who have studied GWI do not believe that it is explainable as post-traumatic stress disorder, yet the Defense Department and the VA often use this category of diagnosis. They also use "unknown illness" as a catchall to deny benefits and treatment to veterans from the Gulf War.

Conclusions of the VA from its research efforts include: "We will never know the cause of GWI"; "There is no unique Gulf War illness"; "We did not keep records" (untrue: records were kept but later destroyed); and "There are no objective measurements." The VA remains noncommittal about the existence and identification of symptoms and their causes. Institutional resistance seems to be a result of fear from potential political fallout of research conclusions.

An enormous conflict of interests prevails. Congress has allowed the Defense Department, the agency that created the GWI problem, and the VA, who is responsible for caring and paying for disability to sick veterans, to work together to investigate their own responses to these illnesses. Perhaps that explains the motives for denial of symptoms, denial of benefits, and denial of existence of any such illness. That would explain the lack of serious research, the lack of accountability, and the lack of trust that veterans are increasingly having from their federal government.

Ross Perot of Perot Systems Corporation, and a long-time veterans advocate, described the breakdown in his January 24, 2002, testimony to Congress. "Instead of dealing with these symptoms in a proper manner using the National Institute of Health and the Center for Disease Control to investigate these illnesses professionally, a group of civilian government employees, with little research experience, was established within the Pentagon and the VA Central Office to direct the research. This was the Research Working Group of the Persian Gulf Veterans Coordinating Board. Over the years, it became more and more apparent that this group's mission, as directed by the Clinton White House and his Presidential Advisory Committee, was to dismiss these serious health problems as stress and ignore these wounded soldiers."

A top clinical researcher from the University of Texas Southwestern Medical Center in Dallas, Dr. Robert Haley, has made promising breakthrough discoveries using a brain-scanning approach to studying Gulf War veterans. Yet the Research Working Group and others in the VA Central Office and the Pentagon have repeatedly tried to impede the research by withholding necessary data, information, and funding.

Progress has been slow, despite a 1994 law granting veterans the "presumption of disability" and George W. Bush's words in an April 2000 pre-election candidate forum, "Our Gulf War veterans should not have to go to elaborate lengths to prove that they are ill just because their malady has yet to be fully explained."[16]

British Study

In the United Kingdom, the U.S. Defense Department funded a British study, the Unwin study, for over $1 million. This provided our Defense Department undue influence and the privilege of corrupting the findings. Concerted efforts diverted attention away from any indictment of vaccines, especially anthrax.

The Unwin study medically reviewed 8,195 British Gulf War–era veterans of the 35,000 British troops deployed to the Gulf, and 75 percent of those troops received the first shot of anthrax vaccine.

"Vaccination against biological warfare and multiple routine vaccination were associated with all outcomes."[17] In April 2000, Blanck, then Army surgeon general, denied knowledge of the Unwin study in testimony before the Senate Armed Services Committee (SASC).

The results showed that Gulf War vets were twice as likely to report chronic fatigue, irritability, headaches, and other symptoms. "Commentary," in *The Lancet* periodical, stated, "Vaccines against anthrax and plague before deployment to the Gulf correlated highly with illness. The investigators speculate that these vaccines, more so than the routine ones given to service personnel, had unanticipated effects."[18] Reports from Britain claimed that one Gulf War veteran was now dying of either cancer or a brain tumor every ten weeks. Overall, Gulf veterans are dying at the rate of 1.7 every month.[19] The British military wisely shifted to a voluntary shot program, in which only about 20 percent of the servicemen took the shot. No British soldiers are currently taking the shot.

Kansas State Study

This study was conducted by Dr. Lea Steele, an epidemiologist and Senior Health Researcher at the Kansas Health Institute. Kansans accounted for 7,500 of the nearly 700,000 American troops deployed during the Gulf War. In 1998, the Kansas State Committee of Veteran Affairs studied 2,030 Gulf War veterans. GWI occurred in 34 percent of Gulf War veterans. Interestingly, 12 percent who reported receiving vaccines but did not deploy to the Gulf had GWI. Whereas, only 4 percent who did not receive vaccines were sick. Vaccines accounted for three times the incidence rate, compared with those who did not receive shots. The lowest service-specific rate of 21 percent occurred with those onboard ships.

The highest rates were found in those who were in Iraq or Kuwait, with 42 percent reporting symptoms. Observed patterns suggest that excess morbidity among Gulf War vets is associated with characteristics of their wartime service and that vaccines used during the war may be a contributing factor. GWI involves a complex scenario, a combination of different things in different people and different exposures and tolerances. Compared with federal expenditures of hundreds of millions of dollars with only unanswered questions as a result, the Kansas study consumed very little time and few resources, two years and $150,000, but made significant progress.[20]

Canadian Study

A 1998 study of Canadian Gulf War veterans accomplished by Goss Gilroy Incorporated, a consulting firm for the Canadian Department of National Defense, found a significant association between receiving nonroutine (biological warfare) immunizations, such as anthrax and plague, and several symptom-defined outcomes, like chronic fatigue, a common symptom of Gulf War syndrome.

French Study

The first French hearing took place on November 2, 2000. Armed Forces medical corps spokesman Colonel (Dr.) Michel Estripeau stated: "France's belief that allied troops were victims of their own protective measures was based on a long series of meetings with U.S. medical experts. About 100,000 of the 600,000 Americans who served in the Gulf complained of ailments that have tentatively been lumped under the Gulf War syndrome heading. No one has yet come to a definitive conclusion, but of 25,000 Frenchmen who served in the Gulf, only 180 have ailments whose origin could be in question. The only really major difference between the groups is vaccinations."[21] We should also consider the fact that French soldiers were not given anthrax and have a very low incidence of Gulf War illnesses.

Common symptoms listed from the 750,000 British, American, and Canadian veterans include fatigue, headaches, joint pains, sleep disturbances, cognitive difficulties, and other physical symptoms.

No Defense Department Study

The Defense Department has not conducted a comparable objective vaccine study of U.S. service members. While an estimated 150,000 received at least one shot, documentation was poor at best. They were told not to talk about the shots to each other after they were vaccinated. Many don't know what shots they received, and because anthrax wasn't mandatory at the time but "highly recommended," it is difficult to conduct a scientific study. After the VA conducted 80,000 physicals among 697,000 U.S. veterans, the Pentagon has finally screened some 40,000 for review. The result so far is that the VA has denied 75 percent of the claims because of undiagnosed illness. These illnesses will remain undiagnosed until further studies are done and the Defense Department is satisfied that a causal link exists between the illnesses and the vaccines.

Update 2002

Results of a study conducted in December 2001 show that Gulf War veterans are twice as likely to be diagnosed with amyotrophic lateral sclerosis (ALS), a fatal neurological disease known as Lou Gehrig's disease. About 30,000 Americans suffer from ALS. Half of Lou Gehrig's disease victims die within three years. Only 20 percent survive after five years, and only 10 percent survive ten years. ALS is an "old person's disease" with an average onset age of fifty-five; however, the Defense Department finds many of its victims around age forty-five. Air Force members were found to experience the highest rates, at 2.7 times the general military population rate. In releasing the results of the study, Department of Veterans Affairs Secretary Anthony J. Principi commented, "The hazards of the modern-day battlefield are more than bullet wounds and saber cuts."

One of those Defense Department victims was F-16 pilot Major Michael Donnelly. Mike flew F-16s in the Gulf War and was assigned to the same squadron that I flew with from Hahn Air Base in Germany a year after I had left. He went from being an all-American, healthy fighter pilot with great hand-eye coordination, to losing almost all motor function, banging his head on a button to type computer messages. Describing his new life, he says that the keyboard is only two inches from his hand, but it might as well be two thousand miles away. Though his wheelchair provides support and mobility, he calls it "my own portable prison."

Tinkering with the unknown, altering the immune system with unsafe, untested, unproven vaccines, could be a ticket for any one of us to join Mike and others down that road. But, there's more to the story that you should know about my fellow "Sabre" from the Tenth Fighter Squadron and the anthrax shot. Yes, Mike was given the anthrax shot. His sister, Denise, told me that he took anywhere from eight to ten experimental vaccines, including anthrax and botulism. No one knows how many anthrax shots he took or what the others were. The Defense Department has lost his medical and vaccination records, as it has for many other Gulf War veterans who are sick. Denise confirmed that there are forty Gulf War veterans who are sick with ALS, but sources tell her that there may be at least sixty-five and probably more.

This initial finding and research is the Defense Department's way of easing into announcing the medical and legal abuses that our troops endured in the Gulf. Denise described the horror on the faces of the first CANG pilots who refused the shot after they met Michael for the first time. Seeing him confined to his wheelchair, knowing that they too could have been there, confirmed for them that they had made the right decision in refusing the anthrax shot.

In 1996, the Presidential Advisory Committee (PAC) on Gulf War Veterans Illnesses concluded that "the issue of accurate medical and vaccination records is central to the concern of many ill veterans. And the absence of records has been suggested by some as evidence that the government is engaging in a cover-up of its own predeployment practices. Had a childhood vaccine been used, the practices noted above would have been in violation of federal regulations. In any event, they contravened standard medical procedures, and possibly Army regulations, which require the keeping of complete and accurate medical records."[22]

It is critical for readers to understand that soldiers who were immunized but never deployed have developed GWI. Those who believed that they had received anthrax were twice as likely to report multiple symptoms as those who believed they were not vaccinated. VAERS reports and congressional testimony prove that the anthrax vaccine alone can cause GWI. And multiple vaccinations have been reported to cause immune effects that result in symptoms similar to those found in GWI. An increased incidence of side effects and interference with immunity are noted in these individuals.[23]

According to the package insert, the incidence of local reactions is 30 percent. The incidence of systemic reactions is 0.2 percent. However, according to one medic who vaccinated 200 service members, 25 percent experienced systemic symptoms and were sent to quarters for flulike complaints. Perhaps, a changed vaccine that is 100 times more reactionary caused these numbers.[24] An illegally modified vaccine with squalene may be at the heart of the inflated reaction rates.

Squalene as an Adjuvant

Startling to discover, Brachman and Friedlander noted that "evidence in experimental animals suggest that adjuvants [a Latin word meaning "to aid"] other than aluminum may substantially increase the protective efficacy of the protective antigen even after a single dose." Were they providing a clue of what may have caused GWI and perhaps laying the groundwork for experiments that have gone on behind the scenes? Eighty years of research has produced a grand total of one adjuvant that is considered safe for human use: a salt called aluminum hydroxide.[25]

The fact that aluminum is the only legal approved adjuvant for use in humans in the United States must be frustrating to vaccine producers and military medical officials who were short of vaccine. Was the Gulf War environment an opportunity for them to test another adjuvant, such as squalene?

Squalene is an organic polymer that has been used as a state-of-the-art adjuvant in at least three experimental vaccines since 1987. In August 1997, Vice Admiral Harold Koenig, then the surgeon general of the Navy, wrote, "The Army has used squalene as an adjuvant in several experimental vaccines ... over the past 10 years." Like every other oil-based adjuvant ever concocted, squalene is apparently unsafe.[26] Also known as an immunoenhancer, it has contributed to Gulf War syndrome. Symptoms include arthritis, fibromyalgia, lymphadenopathy, rashes, photosensitive rashes, malar rashes, chronic fatigue, chronic headaches, abnormal body-hair loss, nonhealing skin lesions, aphthous ulcers, dizziness, weakness, memory loses, seizures, mood changes, neuropsychiatric problems, anti-thyroid effects, anemia, elevated ESR (erythrocyte sedimentation rate), systemic lupus, erythematosus, multiple sclerosis, ALS (amyotrophic lateral sclerosis), Raynaud's phenomenon, Sjorgren's syndrome, chronic diarrhea, night sweats, and low-grade fevers.[27]

Dr. Pam Asa, a Tennessee immunologist, and Dr. Robert Garry, a professor of microbiology at Tulane Medical School, investigated Gulf War syndrome for six years. Prior to studying the blood samples, Asa viewed the gender breakdown of victims. She found that lupus erythematosus, typically a disease predominant among females by a 14:1 ratio, was found in significantly higher numbers of male Gulf War victims.

Testing blood samples of vaccinated veterans of the Gulf War period who had GWI symptoms, Garry found that 95 percent of deployed personnel and 100 percent of nondeployed personnel tested positive for the presence of anti-squalene antibodies. This research suggests that the cause of GWI is neither environmental nor associated with the Persian Gulf. Their research data, published in February 2000, not only shows that the production of anti-squalene antibodies is linked to symptoms of GWI, but also to the presence of squalene in certain lots of anthrax vaccine.

On September 28, 2000, the Hartford Courant reported that the FDA had discovered squalene additives in the anthrax vaccine. This finding directly contradicts repeated assertions made by the Pentagon that squalene is not present in the vaccine. The FDA has not approved squalene for use in vaccines, making this an illegal vaccine.

The FDA did its own tests, using eight lots of vaccine, and all eight lots showed the presence of squalene. Whether or not these lots were used in the Gulf War was not clarified. Previous to the squalene discovery, the GAO had sharply criticized the Defense Department for not doing more to test for the presence of squalene.

When the Defense Department continued to deny that squalene existed, based on a parts per million test, the FDA tested using parts per billion. The result confirmed the Tulane study; squalene quantities found by the FDA were at sufficient levels to cause immune responses in human recipients.

The FDA identified the following lot numbers with squalene: FAV 020, 030, 038, 043, and 047. Curiously, three of the eight lots were not identified. Where are they and what are they being used for? Why did the FDA wait seven to eight months to report this information rather than reporting it immediately after the discovery? Why has the presence of squalene not ended the AVIP, when it violates federal regulations involving experimental drugs and informed-consent requirements?

The Garry research team was awarded Patent No. 6,214,566 on April 10, 2001, for its method of detecting these antibodies. However, Army researchers attempted to discredit the work in June 2000 with a letter to the editor and an article published in the Journal of Immunological Methods in November 2000. That same month, even though the Defense Department replicated and validated the team's research methods, it later applied for its own patent of the same technology on May 18, 2001.

Squalene is found in the human liver, some vegetable oils, and shark oil. Prior to the discovery of the squalene additives, military leaders and flight surgeons responded to the squalene issue by saying, "So what? It's found naturally in the human body." Thinking that no one would have the intelligence or motivation to research the issue, while preventing samples from being tested, the Defense Department must have thought it would be easy to dismiss. True, squalene is safe when swallowed or rubbed on the skin, or at least appears to be. But injecting it into the body is another story. Scientific research links squalene and autoimmune disease in rats, mice, and macaque monkeys.

Individuals who were sick at Dover Air Force Base after receiving the vaccine in 1999 also tested positive for squalene in their blood. The Defense Department refused to test these individuals.

Concern over the relative weakness of the anthrax vaccine, which required six doses, may have enticed the military to use squalene to boost the vaccine's capability. Fears over Iraqi biological-warfare capabilities and overemphasis on force protection may have pushed military medical personnel and commanders to cut legal and ethical corners in pursuing these disturbing paths. Fear is not the best motivation for making sound decisions. Weighing risks in wartime may be difficult, but as Americans, if we are not fighting for principles like human rights, personal freedom, and the rule of law, we should not be fighting. And if we cannot provide for our own citizens what we are fighting for in other places of the world, we are in a sad situation indeed.

The Defense Department may have used squalene to make up for vaccine shortages in the Gulf War and to spread the anthrax mix further. We know, for instance, that by August 1990, the United States had stockpiled only 11,000 to 12,000 anthrax vaccines. We eventually deployed 697,000 troops to the Persian Gulf.[28] You do the math. Now you know why veterans and military personnel facing this shot want the truth. The result of the Defense Department's math shortfall was Project Badger.

For Project Badger, Blanck supervised and organized the production of additional anthrax vaccine at the National Cancer Institute's Frederick Cancer Research and Development Center, located at Fort Detrick. The Defense Department asked more than 160 companies to assist in making anthrax vaccine, but only one said yes—Lederle-Praxis Biologicals of Pearl River, New York. Both Lederle and the National Cancer Institute were unlicensed and unregulated for their roles. The plan called for them to ship vaccine to MBPI (now BioPort) for bottling, labeling, potency testing, and storage. Here again, federal regulations were violated. An IND status should have been applied for and never was.

By December 1990, Project Badger had begun plans to test four other experimental vaccines on U.S. troops in the Gulf. *Vanity Fair* magazine uncovered Project Badger, the equivalent of the physicians' Manhattan Project, and exposed some of Asa's research. Many fear that squalene is still present in vaccine stocks that have been stored or that are currently in quarantine. Of course, the Defense

Department will not allow independent testing to verify whether or not this is the case. The Defense Department claims that there are no impurities. The FDA has consistently proven that impurities, irregularities, and deficiencies exist in this program.

The GAO and Congress investigated squalene as an adjuvant possibility for years. The Defense Department stonewalled to prevent investigation into additives in the vaccine and will not allow independent civilians to test the vaccine. Much is buried under formal levels of "classified" materials, and much will probably remain the secrets of men's souls.

While the Defense Department steadfastly denied using experimental vaccines, it also refused to conduct tests on veterans to validate the findings. Colonel Ed Koenigsberg, the director of the Persian Gulf War Veteran Illness Investigation Team, testified in October 1995 to the Presidential Advisory Committee that no other adjuvant had been used on U.S. soldiers and that no secret immunizations were administered. The GAO remarked about this pattern of deception. Because more than 1,500 service members have complained about side effects of varying severity that they blame on the shot, this avenue needs to be investigated further.

Asa's critics at the Defense Department say that she won't allow them to use her test or that she won't give them access to her data, as though they expect a one-way-street relationship. Absolutely false, she says; she's been trying for four years, unsuccessfully, to get them to give her a vaccine sample. She further states that the highest levels of government don't want squalene to be the smoking gun that ends this program. That is why they aren't more forthcoming on this issue. "The use of squalene as an adjuvant is the 'golden child' for the search for an effective AIDS vaccine…. There are other reasons, dealing with money, fame, and the fact that if the truth ever fully emerges, some medical professionals and military leaders could and certainly should go to Leavenworth. There's the risk of having other unapproved vaccine programs suddenly exposed."[29]

In the November 17, 1997, *Journal of the American Medical Association* (JAMA) article "The Anthrax Connection: A New HIV Vaccine Strategy," Dr. Dennis Blakeslee connected anthrax to AIDS/HIV research and the search for an effective vaccine. We also know that squalene has been used in the development of up to four experimental AIDS vaccines. Could it be that these programs are so deeply linked that even with the overwhelming evidence for stopping the AVIP, it has survived? Were President Clinton's promises for an effective HIV/AIDS vaccine and his declaration of AIDS as a national security threat the driving force for this seemingly out-of-control program? Does elevating the AIDS threat to a national security issue provide a secret, classified program, the necessary legal cover and exclusion to allow government experimentation on the troops? Does a volunteer military imply the surrender of the right to informed consent by the troops, making them subject to military medical experimentation?

When gays were allowed into the military under the "don't ask, don't tell" policy, was it because we were more willing to accept HIV-infected individuals and those with potential for contracting HIV? We didn't have to ask, because annual physicals and HIV blood tests would reveal the test subjects. With a mandatory anthrax vaccine showing signs of promise in fighting AIDS, the Defense Department had an experimental test group in the military that could be used to measure the success of genetically altered anthrax vaccines for fighting AIDS. The non-HIV-infected military troops provided the control group. If the FDA found levels of squalene at measured increments instead of random amounts, this may indicate that the Defense Department is conducting squalene experiments. If the military is being used as experiment subjects once again, no wonder AVIP is so hard to kill.

On July 30, 2001, environmental correspondent Paul Brown reported in the United Kingdom's *Guardian* newspaper that the illness known as Gulf War illness looks likely to have been caused by an illegal vaccine "booster" given by the Ministry of Defence to protect soldiers against biological weapons. In 275,000 British and U.S. veterans who are ill, it seems that squalene may be a contributing factor. The use of squalene was illegal in Britain also. Squalene is not licensed on either side of the Atlantic because of the known side effects. Brown reported that twenty of the veterans were given preparatory vaccines but did not go to the Gulf. All twenty tested positive for squalene, probably from the anthrax vaccine, according to Asa. In 1998, Asa tested five British veterans with symptoms similar to Gulf War syndrome. Of the five, four tested positive for squalene antibodies. Although the British Ministry of Defence denies using squalene, it is being sued for damages by 1,900 British veterans.

Why So Many Sick?

As if that wasn't enough, our Defense Department identified many deficiencies during a March 1992 inspection of BioPort's product quality, including the absence of vaccine stability. This was before the FDA was allowed access to BioPort, beginning in 1993. Significant deviations were found during subsequent FDA inspections on May 4-7, 1993; May 31-June 3, 1994; and April 24-May 5, 1995. The seriousness of those deficiencies was emphasized in a letter dated December 22, 1993, and a warning letter dated August 31, 1995.[30] After repeated promises of corrective action, continued violations were tolerated by the FDA. The FDA inspected the facility again on November 18-27, 1997. Investigators documented numerous significant deviations from the Federal Food, Drug, and Cosmetic Act; FDA regulations; and the standards of MBPI's license to manufacture.

Based on the deviations, the FDA issued a Notice of Intent to Revoke letter on March 11, 1997, stating the intent to revoke the facility's license. After those opposing the AVIP learned of these problems, the Defense Department assured the troops, "These are only minor discrepancies and involve only paperwork problems." However, the specifics show otherwise: failure of the quality control unit to approve or reject all components, drug products, filters, and plastic bags; failure of the quality control to approve or reject all procedures affecting the identity, strength, quality, and purity of drug products; invalidation of the loading patterns and temperature mapping deviations of the air-handling system; failure to establish and follow appropriate written procedures for drainage to prevent microbiological contamination of drug products purporting to be sterile; and the list goes on to cite twenty-three major violations.

MBPI responded with a Strategic Plan for Compliance, presented to the FDA in April 1997, calling for periodic submission of data to the FDA that would serve as evidence of progress toward achieving compliance with FDA regulations. Under this plan, the FDA would review the data and monitor MBPI's progress through follow-up inspections. In February 1998, the FDA conducted a follow-up and found eighty deviations, including but not limited to the manufacture of the vaccine. "Inadequate quality control," "very cavalier," "as if only to meet production quota," "not as if the vaccine would ever be used on humans" were among the findings. Additional problems cited were storage-time and mixing-time inconsistencies, contamination testing, improper filters, potency and stability testing problems, redating of expired vaccines, relabeling problems, and using lots that failed testing.

The inspection resulted in a request by the FDA that MBPI quarantine eleven lots of anthrax vaccine held in storage pending review of additional information to be submitted by BioPort (MBPI) regarding the problems with potency, sterility, and particulate matter contamination, which they called an "inert gasket material." Each lot contained approximately 200,000 doses. A stockpile overview report on July 15, 1998, shows almost 6 million doses quarantined.[31]

MBPI halted production of the vaccine in January 1998 to begin a comprehensive renovation of the anthrax production facilities. The plant closed to meet specifications for sterility, stability, purity, and potency. The FDA's inspection of the MDPH facility in February 1998 found a number of deficiencies, forcing many military members to act for their own safety.

In September 1998, when BioPort purchased the facility, the company agreed to abide by the strategic plan and to other commitments for improvements and corrective actions made by the management of MBPI. No anthrax vaccine has been produced since BioPort became owner of the facility.[32] As of October 2001, only 25,000 doses were reported remaining and available for military use that had not been quarantined.

Another explanation for why so many are sick involves the active ingredient known as the protective antigen. These are particles from dead anthrax bacteria that are used in the U.S. and British vaccines to stimulate the immune system to produce antibodies. These antigens train the immune system to attack anthrax bacteria. However, there can be too many of them. Overstimulation of the immune system can lead to immunological disorders, according to Dr. Jack Melling, former head of Britain's anthrax vaccine program and a consultant to the GAO. "The military had determined in 1991 that the changes they had made [to the manufacturing process with new filters had] increased the potency a hundredfold. The FDA did not know about this until we told them," said Major Russ Dingle, one of the CANG pilots who first refused the shot and resigned.[33] The FDA is slowly getting up to speed on this program, but not without help from Congress, the GAO, and researchers like Russ Dingle, Tom Rempfer, Redmond Handy, and Meryl Nass. The following is a listing of inspections where there existed significant deviation from Current Good Manufacturing Practices (CGMP) as required by FDA regulations.

Inspection Dates	*Action*
March 1992	FDA noted these deficiencies in August 1995 letter
May 4-7, 1993	FDA letter, December 22, 1993
May 31- June 3, 1994	No FDA action at this time
April 24-May 5, 1995	FDA warning letter, August 31, 1995
March 11, 1997	FDA Notice of Intent to Revoke
November 18-27, 1997	No FDA action at this time
February 4-20, 1998	FDA: "The manufacturing process is not validated." More than eighty separate deviations are cited. The Defense Department calls them paperwork problems.
November 15-23, 1999	FDA again says: "The manufacturing process is not validated." Also noted here, BioPort failed to investigate adverse reactions.

"Based on my readings of the 1997 and 1998 inspection reports for MBPI, this is a company that is completely out of control, and they should not be producing medicinal products for human use," said Sammie Young, a retired FDA inspector and supervisor for twenty-nine years.[34] Had he still been employed by the FDA, institutional loyalties and career protection may have prevented Young from making such a statement. The FDA has been the permissive parent-supervisor for the siblings, BioPort and the Defense Department. When it comes to the anthrax vaccine, the Defense Department and BioPort have been unsupervised for so long and so much significant damage has been done that it's hard for the FDA to get back into the game.

Dr. Phillip Russell of Johns Hopkins, former director of USAMRIID, advised against further development of this anthrax vaccine at the National Symposium on

Medical and Public Health Response to Bioterrorism in February 1999. Another opponent of the current AVIP, Russell emphasized the need for a second-generation vaccine, preferably with a purified antigen as one of the ingredients. Once again, with the opportunity to speak freely, unencumbered by institutional loyalties or politics, we can appreciate the honest assessment of an expert.

Sick People, Sick Process

A gross, negligent lack of testing combined with the incapability to produce a consistent quality product may be the cause for excessive, unnecessary illnesses. If illegal experimentation was being done with additives to a questionably licensed vaccine, and thousands were already sick from the shot, there is valid concern on the part of anyone in the military faced with taking it. All questions dealing with these issues deserve answers.

Add the very discomforting quote from BioPort President Robert Kramer, when he testified, "We have the right people doing the right things to get this job done. We will get approval for the renovated facility."[35] Does this mean that the FDA will wave the magic wand and rubber stamp a failed program that does not provide safeguards for uninformed, defenseless future victims of this mandatory program? How safe would you feel as a civilian if you were taking the shot now?

Right now, BioPort is not getting the job done. BioPort did not report to the FDA or investigate the death at Fort Riley, Kansas, of a servicewoman who received her sixth shot. On October 19, 2001, a federal private multimillion-dollar lawsuit was filed in federal district court on behalf of one deceased and one injured soldier. The legal complaint alleges that the efficacy of the vaccine in a mass immunization program for the military was never sufficiently tested, nor were adverse reactions by soldiers accurately or adequately assessed.

Plaintiffs are the heirs of Army Specialist Sandra Larson of Spokane, Washington, who died on June 14, 2000, and Ronda Wilson of Savannah, Georgia, a former soldier whose chronic ill health allegedly resulted from the vaccine. Larson received six injections that almost immediately resulted in adverse reactions—exhaustion, fatigue, skin rashes, pain and numbness in her hands. When the symptoms remained, she was admitted to a hospital, lapsed into a coma, and died twelve weeks after receiving her sixth shot. Larson was diagnosed with aplastic anemia, a bone-marrow autoimmune disease and a serious and rare blood disease, as well as invasive aspergillosis, an infection of tissues or mucous membranes marked by inflammatory lesions where the body's defenses go into overdrive and mistakenly destroy its own tissues. Previously a healthy woman, she quickly went to having no bone marrow, no platelets, and an extremely low count of red and white blood cells. While at the Kansas City Medical Center, Larson was convinced that her illness was caused by the vaccine. She began doing her own research. "Be sure you finish this search for me, because I know it's the vaccine," she said to her sister, Nancy Rugo, also of Spokane.[36] Since her sister's death, Rugo continues to fight for others' safety.

Ronda Wilson, a helicopter pilot, rapidly lost one-third of her body weight and was unable to eat solid foods. She has been diagnosed with thirty-one different ailments, and her doctors no longer know how to treat her. She weighs in at a mere eighty-seven pounds, and she has lost the flying career she loved.

I was honored to share the speaker's podium with Nancy and Ronda in Lansing, Michigan, home of BioPort, at a Veterans Day rally in 2001. Their energy and determination not to give up on this cause was remarkable from the moment we first met and talked together. At the rally, they shared their painful stories and inspired many to do what they could to prevent future victims and to repair the sick process of vaccine development, acquisition, and use.

Air Force Reserve Major Tom Rempfer, one of the A-10 pilots from the CANG who refused to take the shot, recently filed a citizen's petition with the FDA to declare the vaccine "unsafe, ineffective, or misbranded." "Buzz" Rempfer, along with squadron mate Dingle, have exemplified courage, professionalism, and determination in a relentless battle against the AVIP in its current form. Their tireless research efforts, leadership, aggressiveness, and testimonies have gone far in sustaining a battle for truth and ethical conduct in government and in personal safety for military service members.

These examples demonstrate that the anthrax vaccine is unsafe. If only it was an effective shot, maybe we could argue that it was necessary for troops in high-threat areas. However, that also is not the case.

CHAPTER 3

Firing Blanks

We must guard against the acquisition of unwarranted influence whether sought or unsought, by the military-industrial complex.... Only an alert citizenry can compel the proper meshing of the huge industrial and military machinery of defense with our peaceful methods and goals, so that security and liberty may prosper together.

—Dwight Eisenhower

These are the times that try men's souls. The summer soldier and the sunshine patriot will, in this crisis, shrink from the service of their country; but he that stands it now deserves the love and thanks of man and woman. Tyranny, like hell, is not easily conquered; yet we have this consolation with us, that the harder the conflict, the more glorious the triumph. What we obtain too cheap, we esteem too lightly: It is dearness only that gives everything its value. Heaven knows only the price upon its goods, and it would be strange indeed if so celestial an article as freedom should not be highly rated.

—Thomas Paine

An Unnecessary Vaccine

I could not sit still in Indiana. The potential loss of pilots from vaccine-related illness or resignations, the misuse of government resources, and the lack of integrity motivated me to go to Washington.

Lieutenant Colonel Mike Angarole accompanied me. Mike was a fellow 1980 U.S. Air Force Academy (USAFA) graduate and F-16 fighter pilot in a supervisory position in the Madison, Wisconsin, Air National Guard unit. We spent a week together visiting key members of Congress, and met Air Force Lieutenant Colonel Redmond Handy, who gave us support and encouragement. Handy declined a promotion and took retirement rather than take the shot or put himself in the position of having to force others to take it.

The Madison and Fort Wayne units were key units, because the wing commanders of both were arbitrarily trying to speed up the process and give people their shots early. That didn't give us much time to work, only nine months. If we could get help in Washington, we hoped to slow down the process or, better yet, stop it altogether. We presented a briefing outline to several members of Congress and their staffs, the same outline I'd submitted to my wing commander. We explained how the shot was risky for our military and civilian flying careers, how it was a safety issue, and what's more, that there was no guarantee that it would work. Fortunately, we received a different, more professional and objective response from Washington than we had at our home bases with our own leadership.

I had called my immediate supervisor at Fort Wayne when I got to Washington. I told him why we were there, briefly describing our agenda and letting him know we were there as civilians, or as citizen-soldiers exercising our constitutional rights. I'd been back at Fort Wayne less than a month when I was issued a "gag order" directing me to not discuss the shot in uniform with my pilots, and I complied.

A month later, the wing commander tried to trap me into taking the shot by changing the shot policy at Fort Wayne. Now, at that time it was only being "encouraged" for supervisors to take it early. He figured that if I took the shot, the other twenty to twenty-five pilots would follow my example. And if I did not take the shot, he could always punish me, which would intimidate the others to follow his orders. Either way, he would be following orders, so his career was safe. But the "encourage-the-supervisor" policy was not applied to all supervisors basewide. Some were not forced to make a decision, nor were they fired or forced to resign. I did not refuse to take the shot; instead, I insisted on sticking with Defense Department policy, which meant not taking any shots until the spring of 2000. This would give Congress time to examine AVIP, determine its safety and necessity, and proceed with a safe, legal course of action for force protection.

Fort Wayne responded with accusations that I was not supporting policy. I reminded them that Defense Department policy was not to take the shots until one month prior to deployment. The wing commander's early-shot program was of questionable legality, as it was outside of the Defense Department program. The Defense Department, on paper anyway, required a certain FDA procedure and proper administration for the timing of the shots, and Congress was already upset that the Defense Department was violating this set of rules. I told my wing commander that I had no problem supporting Defense Department policy, which I hoped would be changing as congressional leaders became involved. When pressed to take the shot, I repeated that I was uncomfortable taking it while congressional hearings were still being conducted.

I was told that I could no longer be squadron commander but that I could keep flying the F-16. I asked the deputy commander for operations which would be better—to resign or be fired. He said it would be better to resign so that my performance reports and military records would not reflect poorly and my career would not be hurt. In July 1999, after just a few months as squadron commander, I was asked to resign for exercising my constitutional right to speak to Congress. Morale plummeted when other pilots saw right before their eyes the intimidation and vengeance of the AVIP that forced my resignation. Although the leadership had violated whistle blower laws, I planned to let it go. I felt that the leadership needed to have confidence in their choice of commander, who served at the wing commander's pleasure. I turned in a letter of resignation, citing "health reasons." I was intentionally vague, hoping to have an opportunity at a future time and place to explain that those health reasons were for the protection of my troops.

That opportunity came when Connecticut Congressman Christopher Shays of the HGRC asked me to testify after my forced resignation. The committee wanted specific information concerning morale, retention, and readiness. They already knew that pilots would resign rather than take the shot and risk losing their medical certificates and commercial pilot licenses. The committee was examining the safety, effectiveness, and necessity of the vaccine in that context.

I asked Larry Halloran, the general counsel for the committee who extended the invitation, if I would need a protective subpoena. I had already gotten a taste of the retaliation and punishment and I anticipated more. He said that I would not need special protection, because whistle blower laws and congressional involvement would keep that in check.

I was always very careful not to refuse the shot or to disobey an order. This was a legal tightrope for me to walk, which I diligently did with expert legal guidance from several civilian and military lawyers. During this extremely tense time, I was very careful, hoping I wouldn't be put in the position of having to refuse the shot or disobey an order. My alternative plan of action was to resign and transfer to my

USAFA recruiting job, which I had been actively doing as an additional duty for the last five years.

On September 29, 1999, I testified. Of course, this did not go over well back home at the base. On November 24, two months later, the leadership in Fort Wayne grounded me—illegally—from flying the F-16. This came totally out of the blue. I had just flown a sortie that morning and had already flown three sorties that week. My performance was excellent and had been verified by the pilots I flew with. They had seen my performance of great air-to-ground bomb scores and air-to-air kills in a dogfight mission. My fellow pilots were shocked at the obvious vindictiveness of the wing commander.

Being grounded is a crushing blow for any pilot who has "jet fuel" in his blood. But it hurt even more knowing that this was an attempt to prevent me from ever flying again. One of the most precious flying moments of a successful flying career is the "fini-flight," that last flight that caps a career, where family and friends are there to celebrate the great moment. This was a deliberate attempt to inflict pain on a pilot who had enjoyed almost twenty years of service in the cockpit. Because of this illegal punishment and a second violation of whistle blower laws, I filed an Inspector General complaint on January 2, 2000, which bypasses the reprisal chain of command to remedy an illegal situation. The Inspector General complaint was swept under the rug, and two years later it is still there. The Defense Department refuses to respond appropriately to congressional inquiries and is disregarding civilian authorities.

The Defense Department wants members of Congress in its corner on the AVIP but hates having to explain its actions. Congressmen Dan Burton, Christopher Shays, Mark Souder, and Walter Jones have done outstanding work to protect the military with the highest professional, ethical, and legal standards. One of the most interesting moments in Washington occurred when I spoke with Jones of North Carolina a year after my first testimony.

With five military bases in his congressional district, Jones had intensively investigated and boldly represented his military constituents on this issue. He described how the Pentagon brought some of its finest into his office to give him a detailed and classified threat brief to explain the necessity of giving the anthrax shot to all of the military. He described how these Pentagon officials did not even come close to convincing him that the anthrax vaccine was necessary or effective. The threat did not dictate responding with such a risky program, nor did the vaccine provide any proven measure of protection. Based on these two premises, the shot was unnecessary. We were firing blanks at a fictitious threat.

The U.S. Army Medical Research Acquisition Authority, Fort Detrick, summarized this best in a May 16, 1985, document. "There is no vaccine in current use which will safely and effectively protect military personnel against exposure to this hazardous bacterial agent."[1] Despite highly classified Defense

Department Intelligence briefings, many members of Congress were also unconvinced. In fact, in May 2000, Congressman Jack Metcalf sent a letter to Secretary of Defense Cohen calling for "an immediate halt" to this program. Even though the letter was signed by Metcalf and thirty-four other members of the U.S. House,[2] this action had no effect and the inoculations continued.

Pilots who had deployed to so-called high-threat regions were not inoculated in previous years, during the early stages of Desert Shield. So Congress questioned the increasing need to mandate an unsafe, untested shot when it seemed ineffective and, in fact, was unnecessary. The nature and magnitude of the military threat of biological warfare has not changed since 1990, either in terms of the number of countries suspected of developing biological warfare capability and in the types of biological warfare agents they possess, or in their ability to turn these biological warfare agents into weapons and deliver them. Inhalation anthrax is considered by the Defense Department to be the primary biological warfare threat because of its lethality and ease of production and because it is easily manufactured as a weapon.[3] Ten nations have the desire or the capability of producing and delivering bioweapons of mass destruction. They are China, Russia, Iraq, Iran, Israel, Taiwan, North and South Korea, Syria, and Libya. Most experts agree that Iraq does not presently have the capability. However, some Defense Department officers, those tainted by ulterior motives, claim otherwise.

Much of the "threat" described by the Pentagon was scare tactics, perhaps self-serving for the shot program. After all, the British made theirs a voluntary program. Neither the French nor the Israelis have an anthrax shot program. And South Korea does not use the anthrax vaccine, despite its being one of the Defense Department's so-called high-threat areas. There are other NATO and non-NATO allies who do not use the vaccine. They rely on other means: chemical suits, detection capability, antibiotics, and deterrence. When questioned about our allies' policies, the Defense Department arrogantly responds by saying that we do not base our policies on those of our allies or coalition partners. How dare we question the need for this shot?

Inconsistencies with the Threat Logic: The State Department

In the late 1990s, a poorly implemented and wasteful State Department program pre-positioned 8,000 doses of anthrax vaccine in the Middle East. Eighty percent of those doses were sent to eight countries. Later, these doses had to be destroyed when no Iraqi attack occurred and no one took the shot. A State Department fact sheet stated, "We have no information to indicate that there is a likelihood of use of chemical or biological agent release in the immediate future. The Department believes the risk of the use of chemical and/or biological warfare is remote, although it cannot be excluded. Many people believe a terrorist attack is more likely to use anthrax than another country like Iraq."[4]

Under the Clinton administration, State Department employees had a voluntary shot program, even though they were much more vulnerable to an anthrax attack than the military personnel deployed worldwide who were forced to take the shot. The State Department provided its people with information to make their own decisions. Why the disparity in terms of threat assessment? Why are anthrax shots mandatory for military and optional for high-risk government employees?

As we experienced on home soil last year, and as we military types would surmise, a terrorist anthrax attack is an easier scenario to execute than using anthrax on the battlefield. The most probable vulnerability would involve a terrorist attack at home or on a foreign embassy, not a direct attack on our military on foreign soil. The Defense Department agrees, according to a Defense Acquisition Research Project Agency (DARPA) slide: "Most likely first use will be against population centers of ours or our allies."[5]

Doctrinal Shift?
As a matter of strategic policy, any state-sponsored biological warfare attack would be responded to with massive retaliation, perhaps even a nuclear response, as former President George Bush reminded Iraq during the Gulf War. "Let me state, too, that the United States will not tolerate the use of chemical or biological weapons.... The American people would demand the strongest possible response."[6] Today's experts certainly don't all agree on a scenario where these biological weapons might be used, making the necessity of this mandatory forcewide vaccination program appear questionable at best and knee-jerk overall.

But it is extremely significant to note the huge doctrinal shift that has occurred in a short period of time. We are relying on biotechnology to save us in war, and many experts believe this to be a dangerous avenue that will tremendously escalate the arms race. The AVIP tells the world that the United States expects anthrax to be used in war, encouraging other countries to manufacture and produce biological warfare capability for their own troops. Besides, no enemy would be deterred by the United States' decision to use a single vaccine like anthrax. Accelerating a biological warfare arms race by our actions is unnecessary and dangerous. The AVIP fails at the primary purpose of protecting our troops anyway, unless the enemy agrees to limit its use of anthrax strains to those that our vaccine provides protection against. Even if the enemy did us that favor, we would still save only 50 to 90 percent of our troops.

The 1972 Biological Weapons Convention should be sufficient to prevent the production of biological weapons for the 140 nations who signed it. Perhaps a new treaty with real enforcement teeth or stronger verification capability needs to be designed. Iraq has been a party to the Geneva Protocol from 1931, so the world is essentially to blame for applying no sanctions when Iraq used chemical weapons against Iran and the Kurds in the 1980s. By using Iraq to weaken Iran, we may have learned the valuable lesson of not tolerating the use of chemical or biological weapons to solve immediate political goals. We have limited ability to detect impending attacks, so denying nations the opportunity to use biological weapons through enforceable and verifiable treaties may be the only answer.

Joshua Lederberg, Nobel Prize winner and biological weapons expert, summarized it for us. "There is no technical solution to the problem of biological weapons. It needs an ethical, human, and moral solution if it's going to happen at all. There is no other solution."[7] Having the political leadership to make it happen would also go a long way toward an effective force protection strategy.

Doctrinal conflicts and a flawed program inspired this quote from the *Bulletin of Atomic Scientists,* November/December 1998 ("An Unlikely Threat and Bad Medicine for Biological Terror"): "Alternate more cost-effective methods of force protection provide safer solutions for our troops."[8] These might include full body armor. The French military is reported to have the best-designed and most effective equipment. The Pentagon has demonstrated incompetence in this area as well; it has been unable to protect troops with battle dress overgarments. After five years, the Defense Department finally realized that their suits, designed to protect against poison gas and biological weapons, were defective, with cuts, holes, and stitching irregularities. The standard American gas mask had failure rates of 26 to 44 percent. During Desert Storm, the Marine Corps logistics system ran out of replacement filters after only three days.

Stockpiles of antibiotics with an effective military strategy and better detection methods and capability could also render the enemy's biological weapons obsolete. Military planners should emphasize rapid detection, decontamination, and medical treatment after exposure in the event of a confirmed attack.

Fear, Fixation, Hype, Then Panic

Former President Clinton reportedly became fixated on the emerging germ threat and ways to counter it. Influences are said to have included the Iraqi crisis, Russian claims of biotechnology capabilities, intelligence reports, and a novel, *The Cobra Event* by Richard Preston (Random House, 1997), about a terrorist attack on New York City using genetically engineered smallpox and cold viruses. The proposal for the anthrax vaccine was pushed by a small group of businessmen, scientists, and policy makers. They later convinced military leaders and senior defense officials to formalize the program.

On May 18, 1998, Presidential Decision Directive-62 (PDD-62) ordered federal agencies to improve protection and response against biological attack, emphasizing once again what the real threat was: bioterrorism directed at civilian populations. Perhaps a mandatory military vaccination program could work the "bugs" out of the vaccine so civilians could get a safe and effective vaccine quicker. Anthrax shots had ended with the Gulf War but had begun again on a smaller scale in March 1998. Already, by April 1998, the first large-scale refusals of the vaccine appeared onboard the USS Independence, appropriately named for freedom's dream. Ten sailors reportedly refused to inject foreign and potentially dangerous substances into their body.

The grass-roots effort to fight the mandatory shot program began when the mother of a Navy sailor took up the cause after he became ill from the vaccine. One year later, small initial efforts led to the first of four hearings by the House Government Reform Subcommittee on National Security. They reviewed safety, efficacy, and the necessity of the AVIP. One week after the first hearing, on March 31, 1999, in an apparent counteraction, the Defense Department accelerated mandatory vaccinations for personnel spending time in any of the so-called threat areas.

The first Air National Guard unit presented with the shot decision, the 103rd Fighter Wing from Connecticut, lost 25 percent of its pilots. By spring 1999, an Air Force Reserve unit, the 79th Air Refueling Squadron at Travis Air Force Base in California, lost 50 percent of the aircrew in its unit. Obviously, large numbers of pilots were unconvinced of the necessity of the shot. Videotapes and visits to bases by Dr. Gregory Poland to convince the masses of the shot's necessity were ineffective with many pilots because of the hype-inspired, irresponsible statements he made, such as, "Iraq admitted to using bioweapons to the UN [United Nations] and used them against its own people."[9] Wrong! Iraq used chemical weapons only against Iran and, possibly, in the Gulf War. Iraq never admitted using biological weapons.

Full-scale implementation of the AVIP had been announced on May 22, 1998, the same day that the president announced PDD-63, his new counterterrorism policies, in a speech at the U.S. Naval Academy. Months later, in August 1998, White House policy directive PRD-5 seemed to anticipate upcoming problems for the program. In hopes of avoiding congressional suspicion and second-guessing, PRD-5 mentions health, safety, and retention issues that the AVIP might inspire. "Efforts to protect, preserve, or enhance the health of military members may be viewed with suspicion if such measures appear to restrict retention in the military, infringe on freedom of choice, limit personal or career opportunities, pose a potential adverse health effect, or exceed the current civilian norm regarding risk and benefit."[10]

Exaggerating the threat and adding to the fuel of hysteria, Secretary of Defense William Cohen held up a five-pound bag of sugar on television in 1997. He said it was enough to wipe out half the population of Washington, D.C. A group of government experts later wrote in a scholarly journal, *The Archive of Internal Medicine*, that "Cohen's estimate had overshot the mark by 100 times."[11]

In a *Washington Post* article, William Arkin wrote, "When he became secretary [of defense], [Cohen] was halfway through a new thriller on bio-terrorism, a fiction that would influence his view on the one issue that aides and friends say really excites him."[12] In a July 1999 publicity stunt to promote his "baby," Cohen said, "At least twenty-five countries, including Iraq and North Korea, now have or are in the process of acquiring and developing weapons of mass destruction." He stressed, "There is not a moment to lose."[13] One year later, he more accurately stated that at least ten countries have or are developing anthrax as a weapon. A little hysteria thrown in by the secretary of defense is always good for encouraging the military to jump through hoops.

Milton Leitenberg, senior fellow at the University of Maryland Center for International Security Studies, commented on Cohen's aggrandizing and accused him of having fantasies. In a letter to the *Washington Post* on August 14, he said, "They are exaggerated and alarmist. They are probably even dangerous and counterproductive since they virtually solicit and induce precisely what they portray as fearing [a biological arms race and an unstable world because of the biological warfare threat]. No agency of the U.S. government has prepared a threat analysis that provides indications that these events are imminent or even likely. Instead various analysts have provided vulnerability projections and scenarios which are always easy to concoct in the abstract.... Either the advice that reaches the secretary of defense and other senior officials on this subject is extraordinarily poor, or they are intentionally disregarding real-world experience."[14]

The threat was mostly hype coming from just a few key figures. According to Rear Admiral Eugene Carroll, deputy director of the Center for Defense Information, a defense watchdog organization, "I just cannot understand the panic. Without an actual threat of attack and without validating the ability of this company to produce the product, they are spending money on this anthrax vaccine."[15]

The resulting frenzy led to a mistake of blind overambition, when twenty-five teenage Army ROTC cadets at Fort Lewis, Washington, were mistakenly given vaccines.

Prior to 2001, only one person in our nation's history has been killed in a biological terror attack—a school superintendent murdered in 1973 by cyanide-tipped bullets from the Symbionese Liberation Army. A mandatory military vaccination program is an extreme solution. At best, it may be opportunistic, inaccurate, and costly. Regardless, some have found an unprecedented recipe for job security—promote a poorly run mandatory shot program that takes forever to fix and costs vast sums of money, create hype in the media, and scream force protection any chance you get.

It's also glaringly apparent that someone wants increased public attention related to biowarfare and biotechnology at the forefront of military expenditure. The fact that the anthrax strains used in the 2001 terrorist attacks are traceable to Fort Detrick is extremely significant in finding out who is responsible. Among the twenty-seven deadly pathogens missing from the lab are specimens of anthrax spores that disappeared from the Army's biological warfare research facility in the 1990s. Someone evidently entered a lab late at night on numerous occasions to conduct secret and unauthorized research involving anthrax. According to *Hartford Courant* staff writers Jack Dolan and Dave Altimari, as late as 1997, scientists said that security was so lax that entry would not have been difficult.[16] Even the Fort Detrick brass described the lab as dysfunctional because of competitive, personal rivalries, allegations of sexual and ethnic harassment, and recriminations. An earlier article in the *Hartford Courant* stated that "the court record suggests the Fort Detrick facility became a workplace where 'toxic' described more than just the anthrax and other deadly pathogens being handled by its 100 doctoral-level scientists."[17]

In Sverdlovsk, Russia, where anthrax was accidentally released from a biowarfare facility in 1979, even at the ceramics factory pipe shop, apparently right on the centerline of the passing spore cloud, only 10 of 450 workers fell ill and died (a fatality rate of 2 percent).[18] Other sources claim that seventy died. But the hype promoting the threat to our troops does not jibe with real-world experience in many ways.

From that Russian accident, autopsy tissues studied at the Los Alamos National Laboratory in New Mexico showed at least four strains of anthrax. "The purpose of such a mixture," according to scientist Paul Jackson, "might have been to overwhelm the American vaccine."[19] Most likely, that was the case. The Russians had developed a strain that would override protective and defensive vaccines. Russian scientists have reportedly already made anthrax strains resistant to five kinds of antibiotics, which doesn't require much sophistication. They have also made gene-altered strains that could defeat the vaccine, not only ours, but reportedly, their own, which is even more powerful.

Our untested and unsafe vaccine may have been obsolete before it invaded the bodies of our troops. Dr. Ken Alibek is the former deputy director of the Soviet biological warfare directorate (BioPreparat). Alibek, a biological warfare expert, said, "We need to stop deceiving people that vaccines are the most effective protection [method of biological warfare defense]."[20] He told Congress on May 20, 1998, "In the case of most military and all terrorist attacks with biological weapons, vaccines would be of little use."[21] At this time, there may not be effective defenses and medical responses to weapons that already exist, let alone future offensive weapons.

A biological warfare arms race is neither desirable nor winnable. New biological offensive weapons can be developed in ten days to two weeks. Developing effective defensive countermeasures requires anywhere from two to ten years. Plus, there are huge difficulties for the tactical commander on the front lines. Will the enemy assume that we feel protected against bioweapons and create new strains of those bioweapons to try to defeat us? Or will our commander, with an air of invulnerability, make a bad decision to expose our troops, who, because of a modified strain or a noneffective shot, have no real protection? We should not be creating excess hype about bioweapons, when our previous doctrine provided for deterrence. Perhaps doctrine has shifted, intentionally or unintentionally, and we find the AVIP mysteriously justified. If the definition of hype is "creating unusual enthusiasm around thin air," the Defense Department is guilty.

An Ineffective and Empty Solution

There is no documented proof of effectiveness of this vaccine. A memo dated February 6, 1969, from the licensing oversight committee to Dr. Margaret Pittman of HEW states: "The lack of cases of anthrax in an uncontrolled population of approximate 600 persons in the Talladega mill can hardly be accepted as scientific evidence for the efficacy of the vaccine."[22] A few days later, Pittman recommended licensure but wrote: "Clinical data establishing efficacy of the product had not been submitted." So, on November 2, 1970, license approval was recommended to the HEW without any efficacy data. The license was granted on November 10. The FDA had not yet been established to provide civilian standards and proper licensure. Today, we trust the FDA as our watchdog to ensure safety and quality control standards that Americans have come to expect and demand. Astoundingly, FDA inspectors did not inspect the MDPH facility until 1993, twenty-three years after the license was granted.

Demonstration of efficacy was not required by the FDA for licensure until 1972, two years after the vaccine was licensed. In a 1994 paper by Friedlander and Brachman, Friedlander states, "There have been no controlled clinical trials in humans of the efficacy of the currently licensed U.S. vaccine."[23] The paper also claims that the anthrax vaccine is unsatisfactory for two other reasons: adverse reaction rates and lack of efficacy.

Before converting to the pro-vaccine side, Friedlander stated, "The original series of six doses was established in the 1950's vaccine similar to but not identical with the MDPH vaccine."[24] He admitted that they were using the second vaccine, which wasn't properly licensed. He had previously acknowledged the shortcomings of the current anthrax vaccine, including its high reactogenicity and undefined, crude composition. The standard protocol was established arbitrarily at six doses because the vaccine was so weak, which is why the Army had been seeking a better vaccine since 1985. The Army changed its tune later, though, becoming a proponent of the AVIP and claiming that the anthrax vaccine is effective against inhalation of all anthrax strains.

A 1991 Army document noted that "it would be scientifically incorrect to assume that this vaccine would be totally efficacious under different circumstances, that is beyond the parameters of the study design." Only by accepting the assumption that the epidemiological evidence from the original vaccine applies to the licensed vaccine (a big step, considering the differences in the two vaccines) can you conclude that the licensed vaccine is efficacious against cutaneous exposure.[25] But without tests on inhalation anthrax, conclusions are inferences and speculation and not scientifically based.

Often quoted by the Defense Department is a laughable source from the *American Academy of Pediatrics Report of the Committee of Infectious Disease* in 1994 that says, "the anthrax vaccine is effective for inhalation anthrax."[26] The academy removed this ridiculous statement in 1999, probably realizing that not many pediatricians were vaccinating against anthrax in children.

On a USAMRIID briefing slide from October 19, 1995, the Army admitted that "human trials with similar, but not identical vaccine showed protection against cutaneous anthrax; but is insufficient data to show efficacy against inhalation anthrax." As recently as February 1999, the USAMRIID implied that no scientific evidence exists to suggest that this vaccine protects from anthrax in an aerosol form.[27]

Biogenetics experts can re-engineer this vaccine to make it more lethal, as the Russians have proven in their laboratories. And Saddam Hussein, with basic biological warfare capabilities in his back-yard chemistry shop, can modify it in a low-tech manner as well. Antibiotic-resistant strains have also been around for years. There is no known adequate defense capability. Sophisticated or simple methods, it doesn't matter. The vaccine is easy to defeat. Even without the modifications, effectiveness is moderate at best when it is tested against the specific strain used in vaccine production. A secondary issue still unresolved is whether huge doses of exposure could overwhelm any vaccine protection.

For example, news reports as late as December 13, 2001, told how government scientists would be investigating further the way anthrax infects and kills. Government scientists admit they don't know enough about it. With the United States under anthrax terrorist attack, with all the resources available, why doesn't the Defense Department have all the answers now, all of a sudden? Even the lethal dose amount for humans is not defined or understood. Previous estimates range from 100,000 to 100 million spores.

Is It Monkey-Proof?

Authors of the only study to address this issue state that no known surrogate marker or in-vitro correlate of immunity currently exists that allows direct comparison of immunity in humans to that in monkeys. One of the major problems is the lack of a human surrogate or substitute. Rhesus monkeys are arguably the closest similar medical model. There is evidence that pathological findings in the anthrax-infected lungs of monkeys and humans are similar. What is needed today is what is termed a "marker," some signal in the immune defense process that is similar in both species.

In April 1999, Chan said, "Taking all the evidence into account, it's likely that the vaccine does give some protection, but to what extent, against what amount of anthrax, against which strains and how long protection lasts are not known."[28]

The vaccine, however, fails against 82 percent of the tested strains. While the Defense Department says that guinea pig studies against multiple strains are not relevant, it accepts vaccine from BioPort based on potency tests using only one strain with, you guessed it, a guinea pig.[29]

The truth is that monkeys are used in this program when the results using guinea pigs are not what the Defense Department likes. Guinea pigs are fine for testing potency, according to Friedlander. But, the Defense Department uses monkeys for the effectiveness test, or whatever else will give good numbers, even if it doesn't quite understand why, medically or scientifically. For reasons hard to understand, mice have no higher than a 10 percent survival rate; guinea pigs have from a 23 to a 71 percent survival rate. But that's OK; the Defense Department doesn't need valid answers, only tests and studies that show numbers to back up its preformulated conclusions. That seems to be the Defense Department's "scientific" methodology, good enough for our troops with the AVIP. Most of us learned better scientific-method principles of study in junior high school.

Test Results

In a 1986 paper out of Fort Detrick, twenty-seven anthrax strains were tested on guinea pigs immunized at MDPH. The vaccine protected against only eighteen of the strains, but most (more than 50 percent) of the guinea pigs died when challenged to the nine remaining strains. In an unpublished study by Linscott, Fellows, and Ivins at Fort Detrick, in which twenty-four[30] of thirty-three anthrax strains were protected against, again, more than 50 percent of the guinea pigs tested were killed. Obviously those kill rates were not acceptable, but it seems that guinea pigs may have more rights than soldiers, because the Defense Department switched to monkeys for lower mortality rates. In addition, the Defense Department does not consider the "battle-shape" status of the soldiers who survive an attack.

While the Defense Department claims 99 percent effectiveness in the battle-field, what it doesn't tell anyone is that those exposed to anthrax will potentially be incapacitated for two weeks, like the monkeys who, according to laboratory notebooks, survived. How effective is that strategy? We would be making it easier for survivors of the anthrax attack to be overrun by the enemy and become prisoners of war.

The Defense Department likes to tout the Brachman study as proof of the vaccine's efficacy. However, the study was refuted in 1991 in a document written by Anna Johnson-Winegar and P.C.B. Turnbull. Brachman "remains the only one supplying hard data on the effectiveness of the vaccines in humans.... the protective efficacies of both the U.K. and U.S. vaccines are less than ideal.... the injection into human beings of crude and undefined preparations is increasingly regarded as unsatisfactory, particularly, as in the case of the anthrax vaccines, when they are associated with frequent complaints of unpleasant side-reactions."[31]

Here's a comforting quote from Carl McNair of Dynport Vaccine Company of Maryland, which is under Army contract: "The great challenge was to manufacture a vaccine that will be effective against as many as possible of the more than 1,000 known anthrax strains."[32] Good luck keeping up with the biological warfare arms race and 1,000-plus strains. There is no proof of protection against multiple strains of anthrax. And there is no proof that defensive technology, such as an adaptive vaccine, can keep up with the development of offensive weapons. Even if it could, what would that vaccine look like and do to the human body? Would it ever get tested, or would it just be injected again into our handy military test objects?

Vaccines simply are not a cure for the future against military biological warfare. Ensuring that an effective and verifiable biological weapons treaty is in place may serve as the best hope and the best force-protection measure. Considering all the issues and unknowns, it seems that the Defense Department knows that vaccines are a hollow solution. Brigadier General Walter Busbee, joint program manager for biological defense, said, "We need to make the case that anthrax is currently the principal biological warfare threat."[33] In other words, let's invent a crisis and build the case.

The program does not stand on its merits, so pilots in Guard and Reserve units quickly found the nearest exit, without staying to hear the general's fabricated case.

CHAPTER 4

Exit Wounds

The test of leadership: Turn around and see if anyone is following you.
—John Maxwell

An Unpopular Vaccine

By February 2000, all the pilots in the 163rd Fighter Squadron were required to take the shot or be grounded. Like me, they were forced to decide early, and if they didn't make the verbal commitment, they were grounded. Some were even placed on a grounded list without being asked, because someone made an assumption about their anthrax vaccine opinion. The base spokesman must have enjoyed the word games with the media. He told them that the twenty to twenty-five on the list "were not grounded. They just weren't on the flying schedule."

In the end, about twenty of our pilots resigned, quitting or transferring to other units during that six- to nine-month period to avoid taking the shot. This loss made a huge impact on the unit's combat readiness. When it came time to deploy to the Middle East, there were not enough pilots to do the job. Pilots had to be borrowed from other units.

Threats and intimidation were used to try to keep pilots in units around the country. Two of our younger pilots who still owed years of service commitments to the Air National Guard were threatened with jail time, fines, and less-than-honorable discharges. This was after Principal Deputy Assistant Secretary of Defense for Reserve Affairs Charles Cragin said under oath to the House Government Reform Committee, "If someone is going to resign, Mr. Shays, they are certainly not going to be subject to any penalties. That is one of the points of the Guard and Reserve."

Unfortunately, that was another example of false testimony under oath. Neither pilot was given the option to resign. Because they had commitments to fulfill to the Guard, the state of Indiana gave them only two options: take the shot or disobey the order. Both pilots were punished for failing to follow orders to take the shot. I was allowed to finish the last remaining months until I qualified for retirement. Before my time was up, however, the leadership finally lost patience and escorted me to the base personnel office. They watched over my shoulder as I signed my retirement papers. Much to their dismay, this bought me another sixty days until the retirement orders would become effective.

Even more disconcerting to the wing commander, on July 17, three days before I signed the retirement request, the base received notice of Defense Department orders that changed the shot policy. The new policy no longer required individuals to take the shot unless they would be in a high-threat area for more than thirty days. Typically, Guard units don't deploy to places for more than thirty days anyway, without rotating in replacement pilots. This keeps many of them from losing employee benefits from their civilian employers. All the pilots should have been able to come back without taking the shot. So they could still get rid of troublemakers like me, the base leadership cleverly and conveniently kept those change orders for the shot policy secret.

A few weeks later I was informed of the new shot policy from other sources, and immediately withdrew my retirement request. I received written and verbal confirmation from the Air Reserve Personnel Center in Denver that I was back in. I then asked Fort Wayne to reinstate me as a pilot and squadron commander. At that time, the squadron commander position had been vacant since the time I was forced to resign a full year before. The position of deputy commander of operations was also vacant. Having two of the top three leadership flying positions on the base unfilled was a potential flying-safety travesty, certainly no way to run a fighter unit. Nevertheless, they denied my request for reinstatement.

Another outstanding pilot was in a similar situation. Captain Matt Wingham tried unsuccessfully to get back in the Fort Wayne unit when the policy was changed. Once again Fort Wayne seemed to be inventing its own policy, requiring Wingham to agree to take the shot. We were all being punished for not taking the shot the first time around. Only two or three pilots in the unit were originally willing to take the shot. Ten other pilots initially talked like they would refuse the shot, but when the time came, they changed their mind and took it.

Two pilots, Greg Wyant and Gary Pignato, had a change of heart, missed flying, and were in a unique situation, very close to finishing their twenty-year careers. So they decided to go back in after initially transferring to others units. However, the policy had changed, then vaccine shortages forcewide curtailed shots at the base level, and they were not forced to take the shot, even though they had to agree they would. The base offered to get a "waiver" just to help them take the shot but was kind enough, when Greg and Gary told them that they didn't have to go to all the trouble. There was no doubt in my mind, however, that had I come back, they would have found a way to force me, out of pure vengeance and anger, to take the shot. Regrettably, that provides a glimpse of the inner turmoil and divisiveness that resulted from the shot policy even in what used to be a cohesive squadron.

No one who resisted the shot got by unscathed. Wyant, who served as the squadron commander's right-hand man as the operations officer in a full-time instructor position, did a fantastic job for the unit helping us become the first F-16 Guard squadron checked out with night-vision goggles. He was purposely overlooked for promotion a year later, at the end of his career, as punishment, because he delayed taking the shot. Pignato was not allowed to fly F-16s again after submitting his retirement papers, only to find out that retirements were all on hold because of the Terrorist War of 2001. When he questioned the wing commander about whether this was punishment for his delay in agreeing to take the anthrax shot, he was told, "You shouldn't think something negative wouldn't come from it." Resentment for avoiding the shot and grudges have lasted a long time in the Guard. While the shots are on hold for now, punishment and intimidation continue into 2002. These two men were accused of "gaming the system" in front of their fellow service members around the base. Harassment, coercion, intimidation, and punishment escaped no one, unless they quietly took their shots.

It's a sad situation, and it's unbelievable how much time and effort has been spent defending our legal rights and protecting our health against a program spun out of control. We pilots should have been flying airplanes and preparing to defend our country, instead of defending ourselves against an internal enemy. We would have preferred fine-tuning our F-16 skills instead of becoming vaccine experts. Even with the overwhelming evidence against the AVIP, the burden of proof is still on us.

The Air Line Pilot's Association (ALPA) is the largest pilot union, representing 66,000 pilots and 46 airlines. The medical staff of the pilots' union, some with ties to the military, also offered no support, minimizing any problems associated with the vaccine. Dr. Quay Snyder, a so-called anthrax guru from the union's aeromedical staff, insisted that reactions from the anthrax vaccine were essentially nil. He dismissed our concerns and minimized the situation, even when he and I talked on the phone.

Then we discovered that Snyder is a former Air Force flight surgeon who still maintains a blind-faith kind of loyalty about the military. His attitude saddens us deeply because—receiving up to six calls a day from Reserve and active-duty pilots—he was in a unique position to provide true guidance and have a positive impact on safety. We found out later that three of the ALPA doctors had military or government backgrounds, which certainly influenced their perspectives on the AVIP.

In October 2000, I was asked by Congressman Burton to testify for the Committee on Government Reform, which he chairs. I testified twice in Washington, D.C., and two months after testifying the second time, I was hit with a career-ending blow: I received illegal and unsolicited retirement orders in the mail. Standard procedure is for an individual to request retirement. This was an attempt by Fort Wayne or state leadership to force me out in a blatant violation of whistle blower laws, 10 USC 1034, Defense Department Directive 7050.6, and UCMJ Article 92.

This was actually the fifth incident in which military officers violated my privilege of protected communications with Congress. The first was my forced resignation as squadron commander. The second was the insertion of damaging statements into my performance reports. The third was my being grounded from flying the F-16. The fourth was my being pressured into signing retirement papers earlier than required or necessary.

That same intimidation and mean-spirited handling of this program was widespread around the country. I testified to Congress about the devastating effect this was having on morale and retention. I predicted in September 1999 that the Air Force would lose as many as 2,000 pilots if it continued the shot program, and in October 2000, the GAO confirmed that those numbers were a close approximation.

After dozens of pilots had already resigned, one of the general officers, the director of the Air National Guard, General Paul Weaver, testified under oath that there was only one known "refuser." As the director of the Air National Guard, he certainly had to have been aware of the eight or nine pilots from Connecticut and the seven pilots from the Wisconsin Guard who also refused. Their resignations were widely publicized. Many more units had informed their state military leaders and the entire chain of command of their pilots' intentions to refuse the shot. Congress had legitimate reasons for their inquiries, but senior Air Force and Air National Guard officials continued to be deceptive and misleading rather than forthcoming with the truth. They intentionally misled Congress, the media, the American people, and worse, their own troops. This same deception permeated the entire anthrax shot program. Many pilots who quit were disillusioned with the way the leadership had betrayed them and then covered up its actions and intentions with deception.

This lack of ethical behavior filtered up and down the chain of command, even in Indianapolis, where the state headquarters for the Indiana Air National Guard is located. Spokesman Lieutenant Colonel Stuart Goodwin, in a deliberate attempt to mislead the press, told the media that he knew of "only two or three people who recently decided not to continue their careers in the Air Guard, and it wasn't because of the shots." Goodwin knew that was false information, as the leaders were completely informed day by day of the unit's status and of anticipated problems with the shot response. To paint those who refused to take the shot as uncommitted warriors, he used a standard Defense Department tactic to cover up the lie. Speaking for those who left, he said, "These people were thinking about leaving for time issues, spending time with their families."[1] This was not true. Anthrax was the primary reason, but many of those who left would not identify that as the reason because of retaliation.

Intimidation and ridicule were not limited to people who opposed the shot. The media also felt pressure from Defense Department personnel to report the department's spin and to disregard the facts. Goodwin expressed his frustration to at least one reporter involved with interviewing pilots who had reported information contrary to the Defense Department's message. That reporter was quickly reassigned.

The truth was so hard to come by that Fort Wayne officials lied to the GAO when its team later visited the base to survey pilots in person. I had previously met with Dr. Sushil Sharma, the GAO team leader in Washington, D.C., months before. I pleaded with the team not just to survey pilot bases at random but, to ensure that the survey provided valid numbers, to visit units that are immediately facing the threat of the shot and that are well informed about the issue. We also assisted with the survey design. When the team visited Fort Wayne, base officials told the GAO, "Only nine pilots left because of the shot." Depending on how the counting is done and which time frame is used, the truth was that at least fifteen to twenty pilots left because of the shot. Fortunately, in closed-door meetings between the pilots and the GAO, many of our full-time pilots helped set the record straight. They ensured that the GAO team had the correct numbers before they left. Fortunately, the GAO witnessed firsthand the deception and turmoil caused by the Defense Department in administering the AVIP.

The Defense Department's unfiltered tactics, ridicule, and word games extended all the way down to the state and local levels, and its dishonesty must have been the final straw for many pilots. It was really too late for the Defense Department to stop the exodus. Leadership's integrity failure almost outweighed the shot policy's failure. The exit wound at Fort Wayne meant losing more than half its talented and experienced warriors.

According to the September 9, 1999, *USA Today* Weekend Poll, most Americans did not like this program either. Eighty-three percent of the 7,800 polled disapproved of the shot. An *Army Times* poll of military respondents in March 1999 found that 77 percent opposed the mandatory shot. These numbers were consistent with British numbers: 80 percent refused to take the shot in the U.K.'s voluntary program. Thankfully, sanity levels worldwide were not being threatened.

The program was about as clean as being shot with a dirty needle, not only because of the thousands who will face illness and its inevitable expenses, but also because of the ragged scars caused by the damage that was done to so many careers. Many families experienced turmoil over the decision of whether or not to take this shot. It was a threat to family security. I am aware of at least one enlisted person who didn't even tell his spouse about taking the shot.

More than 200 courts-martial were performed. To enforce this program on a nationwide scale required threats of punishment and, in some cases, the actual use of physical force in the military shot lines. Estimates are that 400 to 500 have refused to take the shot nationwide.

Costs

In terms of taxpayer money, the greatest expense was the loss of 260 pilots, representing only 12 percent of the Guard and Reserve units who were faced with the shot decision. The GAO predicted a 43 percent total loss of pilots over the next six months. These pilots quit or transferred out of Air National Guard or Air Force Reserve flying positions to protect their flying credentials and health as pilots, rather than risk it on a shaky shot program. At a cost of $6 million to train each of these combat-ready pilots with eight to ten years of experience, the total cost of this ill-designed program for the United States was $1.5 billion in wasted taxpayer assets. When the total cost of the shot program was only $130 million to administer to all 2.4 million troops, the American taxpayers lost a great deal. The twenty pilots from Fort Wayne alone ($120 million) represented a loss almost equivalent to the cost of administering the program nationwide. What a waste!

But there were also many unseen costs. Friendships, camaraderie, and morale were destroyed at many of these units. Trust in leadership eroded to incredible lows, primarily because of the dishonesty of leadership. On January 12, 2000, seventy-four officers from twenty-five states filed a complaint with the Defense Department inspector general about Weaver's false testimony that there was "only one refuser." A report from that investigation, which was concluded in March 2001, said "his statement lacked the necessary element of straightforwardness, and so was inconsistent with guidelines for honesty. He presented the truth in such a way as to lead recipients to confusion, misinterpretation, or inaccurate conclusions."[2]

The inspector general report protected Weaver, saying he was not willfully false or misleading, and went on to explain how the definitions of "refuser" or "refusal" is so difficult to comprehend. If only they would have helped the general with his definition of integrity. Taken from the Air Force's Squadron Officer School Professional Military Education texts, "Integrity -which includes full and accurate disclosure ... False reporting is a clear example of a failure of integrity.... Integrity can be ordered, but it can only be achieved by encouragement and example."[3] Misdefining or misapplying "integrity" was much more costly than incorrectly defining "refuser," in terms of pilot retention and indelible scars.

Like his commander in chief, former President Bill Clinton, it seems that Weaver did not know what the definition of "is" is. He had difficulty answering about pilot attrition and refusers under oath. However, in follow-up congressional testimony, when asked by Burton what the punishment for lying under oath was, the chamber became quiet. A rush of embarrassment swept through the silent room in the next few minutes, followed quickly by the rancid taste of disgust from what this program had done for the integrity of our military leadership.

On October 26, 1999, Weaver was asked during a nationwide closed-circuit television military briefing why he had said that only one person had refused the vaccine. His response then was also false. He said, "I was very much aware when I said one refusal of a person who had a commitment.... My additional testimony also reflects that I was also very much aware that people did ... did walk who..."[4] Wrong! To that question there was no "additional testimony," period. Nothing close to that was mentioned in his original comments. In an interview just after testifying under oath that only one pilot refused, Weaver contradicted his own testimony, now admitting that a few Wisconsin pilots had walked because of the vaccine issue.

Colonel James Dougherty, Air Surgeon of the National Guard Bureau, who also testified, refused, when asked if the vaccine was effective against all strains of anthrax, to give a yes or no answer. After the third inquiry, he responded, "We believe so." Credibility with the National Guard leadership was devastated by Weaver's and Dougherty's testimony, and the resulting disgust was directly reflected by the pilots who voted with their feet.[5]

The retention nightmare did not happen at every military base with pilots. For example, active-duty pilots had no choice except to face a court-martial or risk losing their health, military career or follow-on career, and family security. They could not easily refuse the shot without paying a heavy price. And many in the military were just not adequately informed about the subject. Some did not want more than a surface-level education on the costs and benefits of the shot, choosing to accept the Defense Department's version of the truth without question, common sense, or practical consideration. It was easier than complicating their lives with controversial information that could lead to confrontation and creating waves. Going with the flow was a better plan for most. Some in Defense Department leadership counted on that type of apathy.

Some were just afraid for their military careers and felt inwardly, without question, that they had to tow the company line. Some blindly accepted all they were told and trusted Uncle Sam to take care of them if they ever got sick from a shot. Ordinarily, that may have been a reasonable belief. This program, like many in the past, proves that it was indeed misplaced trust. And to watch the actions of the military, continually denying any link between symptoms or illness and the shot, with injury case examples in Battle Creek and Dover, should have ended any comfort in the Defense Department's being there to help.

The intangible costs were enormous. Choosing between career and integrity, silence or punishment, some figured that the easiest way out, and hopefully, with a little luck, the safest way, would be to take the shot, hope, and pray. That formula did not work for some. Imagine being put in that position, an opportunity to play vaccine roulette. Your health and your family's financial security are placed on the table as bets for this game. And it's your turn to roll the dice. The military has evolved into something less than honorable when it forces its members into that type of corner.

With more than 1 billion dollars of invested training costs already lost because of pilots who had left, the AVIP was on pace for the Air Force to lose around $12 billion dollars in training costs, not quickly replaceable. The exit wounds were already severe. The Air Force could soon be hemorrhaging the lifeblood of its combat-mission capability. These losses were avoidable and unnecessary. On top of that, the GAO survey predicted that 18 percent of the Guard and Reserve pilots planned to leave in the next six months. The Defense Department's next response was not concern for combat readiness but nonchalantly saying that the losses were not because of the shot program. The Defense Department was in denial and out of touch with reality and its people.

On the day before the GAO report was released, Pentagon officials dismissed the notion that many airmen were leaving because of the vaccine program. "I don't think we've considered it as having a significant impact." said Rear Admiral Craig Quigley, on October 10, 2000. Guard and Reserve pilots fly 50 percent of the missions in the United States Air Force, maybe more overseas; 20 to 40 percent of the pilots patrolling Iraq at any given time are Guard or Reserve pilots—no significant impact? Really! He should think again. Did he mean that the potential waste of $10 billion was not significant to the American taxpayers' wallets? Or did he mean what he said, that they had never considered it at all? In reality, they had plenty time after being confronted with this issue to study and understand it. Now they should be held accountable, with no more deception, lack of concern, or pleadings of ignorance.

How out of touch do you think this guy is? Is the word just not getting to the upper echelons? Are they being told what they want to hear? From all the information we have gathered, they are being told at the highest levels. The logical conclusions are that they don't care about being good stewards of taxpayer resources and are putting their own careers and nest-feathering first; that they're in a classic state of denial; or that they think they can bully this program through and that highly trained, educated, and needed people won't really walk away. I think that the exit polls are ending their doubts on the latter.

The Defense Department claimed that its own exit surveys did not verify those high numbers. What it did not tell Congress or the media was that most bases did not even conduct exit surveys and that the voices of pilots who left were never heard. It did not mention that most exit surveys did not ask specifically about anthrax. It did not say that pilots would not respond honestly to Defense Department surveys anyway, knowing that the Defense Department could not be trusted and fearing repercussions at their follow-on transfer assignments. And it did not mention the shell game, in which Guard and Reserve units rely on hiring active-duty pilots who need a job short term until the commercial airlines hire them, or the practice of borrowing pilots from other units. These newly separated pilots would not put up with the deception and lack of ethics displayed by senior leadership for long, though. Senior officials must have thought that they could play the shell game long enough until their shift was over, with the smell of retirement in the air. The built-in delay for reporting separated pilots and its effect on combat readiness gave Defense Department leaders room to skew the numbers. But the house of cards would topple if the AVIP continued full-force. The Air Force was already nearly 2,000 pilots short the last few years before the AVIP, and pilot training bases were running at maximum capacity. With deployments at a feverish pace and war contingencies on the horizon, Defense Department leadership could only beg from Peter to pay Paul for so long.

Knowing that these games lay ahead, I needed to be able to verify the validity of my numbers, anticipating they would be challenged. To preserve the pilots' privacy, I used encryptions from their initials instead of names, and prepared a chart to show Congress the exact numbers of pilots leaving from a typical Midwest fighter squadron in Fort Wayne. Survey responses from the GAO indicate that out of the pilots who left, 61 percent said that the vaccine program was the main reason. However, if responsible military leadership had been in place, it would have known without exit surveys, just from being in touch with the grass-roots levels of its units.

Some blame can be placed on ignorance and poor leadership. The rest was blatant deception and misrepresentation. Pride and stubbornness were factors—many supervisors in leadership positions just plain did not care about being responsible for taxpayer resources. "If they [pilots] can't follow orders, we don't want them." The wing commander's philosophy at Fort Wayne was that he had a stack of resumes two feet tall if someone was unhappy. He ridiculed pilots opposed to the AVIP for their distrust of their government. And if that was the extent of their trust, he said, they should get out. This missed the point by a mile. For pilots who opposed the AVIP, it was their Air Force as much as it was his. Maybe the wrong people were leaving—the ones with leadership qualities like good old-fashioned backbone, otherwise known as courage, were leaving. However, before any of us left, we tried to fix the problem, which is what any good leader would want. Trying to improve the situation is more valuable than quitting, not trying, or getting kicked out.

According to the wing commander, everyone was replaceable. He mentioned that "rental" pilots from other units were readily available to transfer and fly with us. And this threat was clearly communicated to pilots years before. Never mind that many of these pilots were combat veterans with valuable wartime experience that can't be replaced for at least another decade. The majority had more than 3,000 flying hours, a seasoned and experienced workforce. The unspecified dollar cost in terms of national security, especially adding the failure of leadership on this program, is enormous compared with the already incredibly large numbers on the balance sheet from the mass pilot exodus.

Had the program continued, according to GAO statistics, the cost-effectiveness of this program would have reached extreme levels of absurdity. Talk about the fleecing of America, what an incredible waste of resources. Here are the initial pilot losses in states that were immediately affected.

Actual Pilot Losses

An ongoing informal poll being tabulated by Buzz Rempfer on the Internet shows that more than 700 pilots and aircrew losses could be expected in nationwide attrition because of the shot program.

Connecticut	8
Wisconsin	7
Indiana	21 (over 50 percent of one unit)
Delaware	60 (40 percent from one unit and 50 percent from another)
California	58 (over 50 percent of one unit, one-third from the shot)
Washington	28
New Jersey	20
Tennessee	22 (50 percent of one unit)
Michigan	18

As startling as these attrition numbers are, the cost estimates still don't take into account the expense of training a new wave of pilots. Training time and resources must be considered. Another factor to bear in mind is our country's increased vulnerability, as many of our combat-experienced Gulf War veterans are no longer available to protect us. The combat readiness of units dropped instantly when the AVIP was administered at these bases.

In one case, the pilots may have been saved only by the forces of nature. The only Air National Guard unit flying C-5 cargo planes is based in Newburgh, New York. An estimated twenty-seven of its forty-two pilots submitted letters of resignation to become effective if they were ordered to take the anthrax shot. Mother Nature must have smiled on the pilots the day before shots were to begin at the base. In September 1999, she sent Hurricane Floyd up the eastern U.S. coastline. Even when Floyd was downgraded to a tropical storm, it affected the Hudson Valley and Stewart Air Force Base in Newburgh enough to cause the loss of all electrical power. Emergency generators did not function, shutting down refrigerators at the base clinic that contained the anthrax vaccine. Base personnel were afraid to open the refrigerator, not knowing how the temperature fluctuation could have affected the vaccine and not wanting to release the remaining cold air. High-level discussions between the Defense Department and BioPort officials ensued, and a reckless decision was finally made to administer the potentially tainted vaccine. It would be pure speculation to surmise what happened next, but even with the order to administer the vaccine in place, it is a matter of record that the pilots were not given the shots and that the vaccine was discarded. All forty-two pilots breathed a sigh of relief, and the vaccine was never replaced. Not every base was so lucky.

Lieutenant Colonel Pat Ross is a USAFA graduate, an A-10 Squadron Commander from Battle Creek, Michigan, and a good friend and commercial pilot. In a six- to eight-month period in 1999, he lost almost 50 percent of his pilots. Pilot safety was Ross's major concern. However, "ongoing punishment and coercion" was also extreme in Battle Creek from the beginning, when the first three seriously sick individuals testified to Congress. Combat readiness was becoming a concern for supervisors, who were left to pick up the pieces.

Reservists around the country, who also work as commercial pilots, had reported symptoms, such as chills, dizziness, and fever, that they attributed to the anthrax vaccine and that necessitated sick leave. The GAO pilot survey report gave a further breakdown of how people felt at the grass-roots level about shots and safety. Below is a summary of the results; the survey had a 95 percent confidence rate.[6]

The GAO Report

- 74 percent believe that immunizations in general are effective [so it's not a fear or distaste for shots in general].
- 60 percent believe them to be safe.
- But, 65 percent report little or no support for the anthrax vaccine program.
- 76 percent would not take the shots if they were voluntary. This compares to the 80 percent of British who refused, and the 83 percent of Americans who believed that this should be a voluntary shot.
- 87 percent say they would be concerned if other vaccines were added to the program, as the Defense Department already plans under the JVAP.
- 42 percent have already taken one or more shots.
  Within this 42 percent:
    - 86 percent report having experienced some type of local or systemic reactions.
    - 71 percent filled out no VAERS forms to report symptoms [presumably for fear of repercussions and job loss].
    - 60 percent did not discuss their symptoms with military health care officials, fearing loss of flight status.
    - 49 percent feared ridicule from the intimidation and strong-arm tactics used by the military for this program.
    - Only 6 percent reported symptoms using VAERS.
    - 10 percent had swelling in the arm for more than seven days.
    - 6 percent experienced extreme fatigue.
    - 7 percent had joint pain lasting more than seven days.

Total loss estimates of 1,500 to 2,000 pilots were right on track if the vaccination program continued, according to the GAO. This number, the GAO's testimony, and the report given to Congress were especially gratifying for me, because in my testimony a year earlier, I had predicted that 1,000 to 2,000 pilots would be lost if the AVIP continued. Now we had proof. Now the public and Congress could hear the truth, instead of the Defense Department's spin and distortion.

The Defense Department's presentation of the AVIP, to whatever audience, consistently raised serious ethical concerns for many pilots. A prime example came from the CANG pilots. After forming a Tiger Team to research for their commander, the pilots there, led by Dingle and Rempfer, searched in vain for veterinarians who had received the vaccine, as the Defense Department had claimed. No medical school, no veterinary school, neither the Peace Corps nor the sheep ranching organizations, knew anything about such a vaccine. Calls to at least two African nations revealed no further clues. Contrary to repeated Defense Department assertions that the veterinarian community received anthrax vaccines on a repeat basis, Dr. Bradford Smith, a veterinary professor at the University of California-Davis, said in March 1999 that he knew of few veterinarians that were taking the vaccine.[7] If the Defense Department could not tell the truth about such a simple fact, what more were they hiding behind the AVIP? Most pilots did not want to find out when it was too late.

The AVIP quickly proved for pilots who left that it was a combination of factors that were demonstrated in this debacle that disillusioned them. It wasn't just that the shot was untested, unsafe, and unnecessary. For some, it was the violation of a Code of Ethics that would dissolve their military relationship. For some, who fought in combat for the country they loved and served, Duty, Honor, and Country felt betrayed by leadership that would compromise their honor. The AVIP's other symptoms, unpopular and unwise, were illustrated loud and clear by the mass pilot exodus. The disgraceful ethical conduct displayed by senior military leadership was a major factor in tipping the scale. In his citizen's petition that Rempfer filed with the FDA, he said, "The military leaders' lack of integrity was leaving an indelible stain on the integrity of the U.S. military."

Their behavior and the AVIP's record will be focused on next.

CHAPTER 5

Our Trust Is Shot

Integrity First
Service Before Self
Excellence in All We Do
—United States Air Force Motto

The only thing necessary for the triumph of evil is for good men to do nothing.
—Edmund Burke

An Unethical Vaccine

The Medical Profession's Oath of Hippocrates: "First do no harm."

The Hypocritical Oath: "Support a person, program, or personal career rather than supporting and defending the Constitution of the United States against all enemies foreign and domestic."

Air Force Captain John Buck, a doctor and the acting director of the emergency room at Keesler Air Force Base, Mississippi, faced a military court-martial in May 2001, rather than take the shot. He was willing to deploy to an overseas threat area or sign a waiver releasing the military from liability if he could be excused from taking the shot. A fellow officer and friend had warned him, "Whatever you do, don't take that vaccine." This friend went from one of the top 10 percent of the physically fit to someone who could barely get out of bed in the morning" after completing the series of shots.[1]

Upset with the haphazard way that troops were vaccinated in the Persian Gulf in 1998, Buck became vocal. Some troops got sick, others were punished if they refused, and some were able to escape the shot because it was administered so poorly.

Buck said, "Medicine is founded on three principles: trust, science, and patient rights. And so if I simply turn my head and ignore the rights of my patients, I have compromised my trust. This vaccine is not founded on good science. So this program violates all three of those principles."[2] Patients who showed no symptoms before the shot later developed serious symptoms like thyroid disorders, autoimmune disorders, and chronic fatigue.

The result of Buck's court-martial was that he was allowed to remain in the military. And fortunately, he will not serve prison time for disobeying a direct order to take the anthrax vaccine. After ninety minutes of deliberation, an eleven-member panel of Keesler Air Force Base officers sentenced him to sixty days of base restriction; fined him half his salary, $1,500 per month for fourteen months ($21,000); and ordered that a written reprimand be placed in his personnel file. Lieutenant Colonel Mark Allred served as military judge in the case.

Buck's lawyer, Frank Spinner, challenged the judge's refusal to accept documents questioning the safety of the shot, its effectiveness, and the lawfulness of the order. Buck was denied due process of law. It's ironic that Buck would have died so that others on foreign soil could know such precious rights. But his own military, and his own country, denied him the same rights that they granted to other citizens. He was not allowed to argue that the vaccine was an experimental and possibly hazardous drug, unlawfully forced on the troops; the defense was prevented from using expert testimony from the GAO's Dr. Chan.

Spinner did question Lieutenant Colonel John Grabenstein, the Army AVIP agency deputy director, about his credentials as a pharmacist to make judgments about the legal status of the vaccine. Interestingly, Grabenstein said that extra tests were not required for the vaccine lot that Buck would have received. However, that specific lot was required by the secretary of defense to undergo additional testing. It seems the lieutenant colonel must have felt empowered to overrule the secretary of defense that day. Spinner also asked Allred at one point if he was influenced by outside authorities, presumably to guide the direction of this "mock-trial." Allred did not respond.

When I met Buck on February 12, 2001, I was impressed with his demeanor, his professionalism, his love for both the Air Force and his country. The suffering he described seeing in his patients also gripped my life in the same way, and I dedicated myself to trying to prevent future victims. Because of the position I was privileged to be in, I felt that it was my duty to protect, initially, my pilots and later, servicemen everywhere, especially those without much of a voice on this issue. Our enlisted force and those on active duty, where I served for almost nine years, needed an advocate. Unfortunately, preventing those injuries in the short term would not be possible for either one of us.

It was the summer of 2000, a few months after my unit at Fort Wayne was forced to take the shot for its deployment to Saudi Arabia. I returned home from my civilian airline trip to a disturbing message. The message was from one of my many enlisted friends, a female administrative troop. She had been healthy and fine before the shot but had complained of chronic fatigue and constant aches afterward. In her message, she told me that she had been diagnosed with Grave's disease and was now sentenced to steroids for the rest of her life, with tumors on her thyroid and a resting heartbeat at the time of 152 beats per minute. I remember listening to that voicemail while driving in my car, my heart gripped with anguish. Tears of futility poured from my eyes and forced me to pull over to the side of the road. The thought crossed my mind: Had I failed her? Could I have done more? It's human nature to question ourselves in such circumstances. However, unlike many of my superior officers in the military, I could still sleep well at night. And I could face the troops I served with mutual trust and respect, knowing that I had sacrificed for them and had done all that I possibly could and that I had remained true to my oath of office.

If we had a hundred generals like Buck, with his courage and conviction, the military would be infinitely better served. I had to wonder, though, where the support from our country's leaders had disappeared to. Where was the voice of Senator Trent Lott of Mississippi, Buck's state of residence, and his support on this issue, especially considering Congress' knowledge of the repeated abuses by the Defense Department's military medical community.

Perhaps these leaders agreed with one of Indiana Senator Evan Bayh's staffers, who responded at one of our meetings before the troops at Fort Wayne took their shots: "The military gives up all their rights when they join." Do all Americans believe that we give up all our rights to serve in the military? Is that the attitude of gratefulness I should expect from a nation I was willing to die for? My close friends, classmates, and fellow pilots who died in peacetime preparing to defend this nation in future wars - did they have any idea that their ideals and personal rights were so easily betrayed and trampled on?

Some civilians may be clueless about the Constitution that we serve or the human rights that we defend around the world. But I had difficulty accepting that the military would once again betray many of its own for its image. Perhaps our civilian leaders who cannot relate to the concepts of military sacrifice and service are so busy running the country or hearing from America about every issue except protecting their own sons and daughters that we are beyond hope. And when military members entrust commanders to be stewards or trustees of their rights, we are vulnerable to the abuse of power and command position. Military members are not second-class citizens when it comes to basic human rights and constitutional rights.

As the media is now illustrating for the public on their living-room televisions, there is a double standard. Postal workers who are afraid of contracting anthrax are taking an "experimental" vaccine and are being given informed-consent privileges. The military, taking the same experimental vaccine for a purpose never tested or authorized on the product label, is not being given the same privileges. The AVIP is a betrayal of trust when it comes to a commander's responsibility to be a good steward of the rights of his troops. Buck understood that principle of trust better than most.

Lott did offer a summary for his media spot: "Dr. Buck stood on principle. And it is unfortunate the Air Force is prosecuting him."[3]

No, Senator Lott, it's unfortunate that the American people and our country's leadership did not stand for principle alongside him.

On May 3, 2001, Air Force Major Sonnie Bates and Buck filed suit in U.S. District Court for the District of Colombia asking that the vaccine be declared an "experimental drug" and thus prohibited without service members' informed consent. Violating laws in the name of following orders is reprehensible to most professional military officers and not a legal defense.

"Following orders," as the courts have ruled, "is also no excuse for unethical conduct, even in combat." As in the case of Lieutenant William Calley Jr. and the My Lai massacre in Vietnam, many officers have been tried in the courts and punished because they issued or followed illegal orders without questioning the legality of the orders they were given.

During one of my discussions with my wing commander at Fort Wayne,

I brought up the example of Calley's illegal and unethical orders. I was told with a laugh of disgust that there was no connection between that and this shot program. Many officers might disagree, considering the fact that following orders is not an excuse to violate the law, either for Calley or for us. Calley killed innocent foreign civilians in wartime, a punishable crime. The AVIP killed our own troops in peacetime, violating international standards of legal and moral conduct.

One of the greatest leadership and ethics laboratories in the world is at the U.S. Air Force Academy. Students and instructors there participate in character development studies and scenarios of ethical conduct in preparation for real-life situations. The AVIP is a perfect case study for grooming future leaders on resolving ethical and legal questions in military policy issues. Critical lessons need to be learned from this unethical vaccine and its effects on the military's morale, retention, and readiness and the future integrity of our leadership.

Major Rempfer (a 1987 USAFA graduate) and Major Dingle, A-10 pilots in the CANG, resigned from the Guard after completing their Tiger Team research assignment for their commander and refusing to take the anthrax vaccine. Dingle and Rempfer played key roles in opposing the AVIP and seeking to promote integrity in the force-protection process. The two pilots filed an Inspector General complaint against two senior Army officers, Lieutenant General Blanck, a former Army surgeon general, and Colonel Friedlander, an Army medical supervisor who was involved with vaccine testing. They provided separate testimonies before a military court in Canada and the SASC, and both misrepresented the status of the license application in order to cover up the significance of its questionable nature.

The inspector general's office attempted to dismiss the complaint, until pressure from Congressman Shays prompted its re-examination. The inspector general conveniently determined that the complaint should be forwarded to and investigated by the same Defense Department office that supports and lobbies for the AVIP. How's that for an objective, independent review and investigation?

Blanck told the SASC in April 2000 that a 1996 license application for another protective use of the vaccine (inhalation) "is really for the new BioPort manufacturing facility, not for the vaccine per se." However, Kim Root, a spokesman for BioPort, testified that the 1996 vaccine license application was not a part of the application for a new licensed facility. Had Blanck honestly informed the senators about the new license application, it is highly likely that they would have investigated further why the current vaccine license was inadequate. When asked directly by Senator John Warner about whether anthrax was a "state-of-the-art" vaccine, Blanck said, "Yes, sir. This is a current vaccine, meets all the standards; it will protect against all natural strains."[4] Perhaps, he also suffers from memory loss from the vaccine or from the definition of "is" syndrome.

On March 30, 2000, at a court-martial for a Canadian soldier who refused to take the vaccine, Friedlander testified before Canadian Military Judge G.L. Brais. In grossly evasive fashion, he denied knowing anything about the manufacturer's new license application, even though the program is supervised by the Army medical office where he works. He also refused to concede that the vaccine was licensed only for skin exposure to anthrax. However, in a October 20, 1995, briefing, he presented the fact that there was insufficient data to demonstrate protection against inhalation disease. A briefing slide from that meeting explained that an IND application that was prepared by the Army was for protection against inhalation anthrax. Minutes from a February 9, 1996, meeting confirm his direct knowledge of the limitations of the current vaccine. On November 10, 1997, Friedlander officially confirmed a third betrayal of his own testimony when his briefing slide showed that one of the three changes being sought included the use of the vaccine for inhalation anthrax.

No amount of lawyering or wordsmithing could instill confidence in the troops who keenly watched the performance of these generals under oath. Their leaders would so quickly sacrifice the future health and human rights of their men as pawns on the chessboard of biological warfare and experimentation. The testimonies of these men bring great discredit upon themselves, the United States military, and the United States of America. Worse, implementation of this illegal order resulted in up to 500 punishments and discharges, more than 300 discharges of Guard and Reserve pilots, and nearly two-dozen imprisonments of enlisted members.

After investigating Gulf War illness, Senator Richard Shelby described "the apparent aversion to full disclosure by DOD…. [We are] constantly challenged by the department's evasiveness, inconsistency and reluctance to work toward a common goal here."[5]

Blanck did tell the truth in early 1999, speaking of the undercurrent of distrust of the government and the military. "Clearly we have a credibility problem."[6] And he was right. When the foundations of the AVIP are not based on truth or medical science and its implementation is grossly mismanaged, then defended without integrity, a huge credibility gap emerges.

Why Lie?

One wonders why Defense Department officials simply refused to tell the truth, even under oath. Why would they dishonor themselves, their profession, and their military branch to protect a program? What honor was there in that? Fine, if they believed the shot to be safe; but why not tell the truth so Congress, the troops, and the citizens could draw their own conclusions and take appropriate action for themselves and their own safety?

Members of Congress at the hearings were frustrated and disgusted. Their questioning of Defense Department leadership had to be perfectly phrased in order to yield truthful and straightforward responses. Military members and citizens were appalled and offended to witness these lies at congressional hearings over and over again. There was no proof, no documentation, only unsubstantiated, vague, and over-reaching claims and repetition of the party line. While that may be useful under interrogation as a prisoner of war, it was a crime and a disgrace for citizens and observers to witness. One congressman used the word "disingenuous" to describe their word games and evasiveness.

The Defense Department's continuing state of denial forces it to defend a program rather than to tell the truth under oath or work toward solving problems in the program. Illustrating the denial are its claims that the sick are disloyal, as if they were a threat to the Defense Department's image. Accountability and responsibility for the AVIP or any policy is so vastly spread, why do Defense Department officials feel such personal stakes to defend it at extreme costs of personal integrity? Why not simply tell the truth? Successful, strong military forces require uncompromising integrity and unity. Unity requires that loyalty saturate the chain of command in both directions. Loyalty must be nurtured in truth, respect, and trust, then extended through all levels of command to support the individual soldier. The AVIP represented a betrayal of trust to most of us at the grass roots.

Just as the World Trade Center was a monument to much that is good in America, truth and trust are monumental pillars for military strength because they lead to essential qualities of integrity and loyalty. While serving as a liaison officer for fifteen high schools and about 10,000 students for the USAFA, I remember concerns popping up from time to time about the quality of candidates, from a values and character standpoint, that we were sending to Colorado. Our recruits certainly reflected the standards of our society. Many worried that an erosion of values and character could eventually be damaging for our future military institutions. However, perhaps the focus should not have been only there. Considering the moral standards that Washington was being exposed to during the birth of the AVIP, some fundamental cracks may have made us vulnerable where we least expected it. Just as the World Trade Center took blows at its upper levels and collapsed, our military's senior leadership on this AVIP issue did not check-six and keep strong the pillars of truth and trust.

Truth became the biggest casualty in this program. And that's the sad truth. A Pentagon-sanctioned survey of Army and Marine Corps personnel found that only 35 percent believe what their service leaders are telling them and that only 44 percent think their leaders would make tough, unpopular decisions.[7]

Inspector General complaints were filed by seventy-four rank-and-file against a general officer who lied before Congress. Of course, the inspector general could not hammer one of his own, so the result was a candy-coated version of what the general meant to say. Fortunately for him, the times fostered a mentality of tolerance and allowed the general to skate and avoid jail. However, members of Congress who were deceived or misled - whatever the politically correct word for lying is - were not extremely happy about it.

Heavy-handedness

One of the common character assassination techniques was, "Well, who do you think knows more about the threat, some general (or the secretary of defense) with thirty years' experience or a pilot?" Or, "Who knows more about vaccines, a doctor or some pilot?" The fact is that many of the pilots were more educated, wiser, more experienced in battle and high-risk threat areas, and smarter about this vaccine than any of them. And many were more tested and better trained in ethics-challenging scenarios and leadership laboratories. Pilots were not influenced by empire-building, political agendas, greed factors, or career enhancement with respect to the AVIP; they just wanted to fly airplanes. They were still doing what they'd always done. Being the quality officers and top-notch pilots that they were, they were also checking-six with the AVIP. Unfortunately, checking-six for the AVIP meant being sure that the military leadership didn't stab you in the back, rather than watching out for the typical enemy.

To administer, enforce, and perpetuate a program like this one, which is unethical at its core, required deception, threats, coercion, and unfair punishment. Preventing evidence from being presented to military judges intent on perpetuating the crimes and public ridicule or character assassination of those who spoke out were standard tactics. The Uniform Code of Military Justice (UCMJ) was used to punish refusers and to intimidate those who opposed the vaccine. They were labeled as malcontents, conspiracy theorists, and paranoiacs; the intelligence and courage of those with legitimate questions were ridiculed; they were called "a vocal minority who think the battlefield is where a farmer works" and "Gortex is one of the Power Rangers."

Character assassinations and ridicule were the norm for the Defense Department's defense of the AVIP. With an appeal to emotion and logic, its best attempt at a sound bite for public relations was, "We wouldn't want to send Johnny into battle without a helmet, would we?" meaning, "See how nice we are protecting Johnny? It's only common sense for him to wear his helmet to protect his pretty little head. And we can't have Johnny questioning why he should wear a helmet, can we?"

To reduce this program to such a simplistic argument or to compare it to something Johnny wears is an insult to intelligence. Most Americans see through that ridiculous manipulation. The grass roots of the military contains highly educated and trained doctors, lawyers, pilots, officers, and enlisted members with extensive experience and education, and they were not so easily fooled as Defense Department leadership apparently believed they would be. The majority of the military overwhelmingly believed, four to one, just like civilians, that mandating the injection of a potential poison into the body, without proper safeguards or warnings of the dangers, was wrong and was completely different from putting on an overgarment.

Secretary of Defense Cohen added confidence to the AVIP by saying, "No third eye has emerged" (he was evidently speaking of himself after taking the shot). Adding another irresponsible comment, one military doctor said, "It just increases your sex drive." Pentagon spokesman Ken Bacon, an expert on "spokesman-ship," offered his expert medical opinion, saying, "It's safe and reliable.... It works and has no side effects." Finally, Rear Admiral Michael Cowan, the medical readiness director on the Joint Staff, said, "The side effect percentage is something like .00002 percent, which makes it many times safer, for example, than the diphtheria shots we give our children." Obviously, he was not a math major, throwing around dubious numbers like that. And here are some numbers he forgot when he offered the suggestion of comparing the anthrax vaccine to the diphtheria vaccine. Since 1989, the United States has paid $839 million to 1,100 diphtheria claims in a special no-fault federal vaccine court.[8] Maybe his comparison is an omen of the AVIP's success. Or, what about the flawed swine flu vaccine of the 1970s that cost the government $92.9 million in payouts to injured vaccine recipients?

Despite having exemplary records, those opposed to the AVIP were questioned for their commitment and branded as unwilling to deploy to the Gulf. In a brilliant display of professionalism, the commandant of the Marine Corps, General Charles Krulak, said that refusers, "are petrified their penis is going to fall off." He went on to say that the vaccine was the safest ever given to American citizens.

I guess they thought that "tough love" wouldn't work for macho troops, so let's "beat them into submission." "Most of these folks have never spent a single moment in harm's way and have no appreciation of what that sacrifice means," according to Major Guy Strawder, former director of the U.S. Army AVIP, as posted on its Web site[9] from June to October 1999. Insulting comments like that from "shoe clerks" (nonpilots) only made war-veteran pilots, who have spent countless hours in harm's way, happier to leave.

One gentleman who spent time in harm's way getting the shot for Major Strawder was National Guard Master Sergeant Thomas Starkweather. He became sick right after his fourth shot with vomiting, night sweats, diarrhea, and memory loss. He is a perfect example of the breakdown in trust. Army medical doctors told him that he simply had the flu. Starkweather requested an evaluation from Walter Reed Army Medical Center, but that was denied. He was told to continue taking the anthrax shots, a violation of Defense Department policy. Major General E. Gordon Stump further minimized this man's illness, saying he showed no symptoms or signs associated with anthrax. The icing on the cake is his shot record.

He was given the vaccine on March 15, 1999. The lot or batch for his shot, FAV030, had expired the month before, on February 23, 1999. Written clearly over the top of that date, someone at the base had altered the expiration date to March 16, 1999. They told him it was a clerical mistake and directed him to turn in any copies of his shot record, which he refused to do.

There were numerous verifiable reports where BioPort, acting through the Defense Department, had redated vaccine lots in order to continue using them. Redating by a manufacturer beyond the expiration date is a violation of the Federal Food, Drug, and Cosmetic Act and shows blatant disregard for federal laws.

The HGRC stated: "Trust must be earned. It can be earned only with a degree of candor and openness that has not been the hallmark of the AVIP to date. The Pentagon still refers to absolutist declarations, heavy-handed propaganda, and ad hominem attacks where the risks of the anthrax vaccine are communicated too effectively or persistently." Evidently, those heavy-handed tactics are used by the Defense Department not just on its own military troops but also on the FDA and BioPort. This triangle of codependency made for a strange relationship among the three.

In a February 22, 1999, e-mail, a Pentagon official discusses how other agency supervisors were urging the FDA and BioPort to release lots that had been held up for scrutiny by the FDA.[10] The e-mail from U.S. Army Brigadier General Eddie Cain, an anthrax supervisor, now retired, was seen by Dr. Michael Gilbreath, a civilian Pentagon biological defense employee. Threats that the Defense Department would circumvent BioPort and contact the FDA were indicative of the department's aggressive nature behind the scenes. This e-mail from Cain to Army Colonel John Wade predicted that Shays would be upset by the Pentagon's influence over the FDA. "If you think Congressman Shays was critical of the current relationship between FDA and the DOD, wait until he finds out that DOD is calling the shots on-sight."[11]

Cain's e-mails also provide some insight on the court-martial trial of Buck. The judge kept Chan's testimony out of court, because Chan could confirm that the vaccine used in the military's mandatory shot program was different than the one used in the Pentagon's studies of anthrax effectiveness. And he could testify that the Defense Department did not mark the shot records from the Gulf War of personnel receiving the vaccine, enabling him to rebut the Defense Department assertion that there was no causal relationship between Gulf War illness and the shot. Writing in that context, Cain said, "We are digging ourselves a hole that will be too difficult to crawl out…[of and could be]…big-time trouble."[12]

According to findings from the Senate Veteran Affairs Committee in 1994, for at least fifty years, the Defense Department has intentionally exposed military personnel to potentially dangerous substances. This trust and loyalty has been broken many times in the past. As Handy noted, the "DOD has repeatedly failed to comply with the required ethical standards when using human subjects in military research during war or threat of war."[13]

Likewise, with the AVIP, again, the Pentagon misled the American public regarding an independent review in 1998. The secretary of defense required this independent review for the AVIP. However, it was conducted by someone with no expertise in anthrax purely to provide general oversight of the vaccine program. Based on the positive report by Dr. Gerard N. Burrow of March 2, 1998, the vaccine program was implemented.

However, Burrow, a gynecologist, later acknowledged that he "accepted out of patriotism." He did not accept, however, an invitation to explain his role or expertise to a congressional committee. Instead, he sent a letter. According to his letter to Shays on April 26, 1999, "I was very clear that I had no expertise in anthrax and they were very clear they were looking for general oversight of the vaccination program."[14] It was purely a public relations tool, a sham. With that "expert" independent review, the military justified continuing to give the shots.

Missing the Four-Point "Shot": A Four-Point Schmooze

Following is the Four-Point Review, preconditions announced in December 1997 and mandated by the secretary of defense before implementation of the AVIP. It required:

1. *Review of the health and medical aspects by an independent medical and scientific expert.* However, to make a mockery of this point, only a cursory view was given by Burrow.

2. *Supplemental testing of current lots in stockpile to ensure safety, potency, sterility, and purity.* Because of safety issues from FDA discrepancies, this testing was meant to add confidence. Testing could not repair the fact that potency varies by a factor of forty from lot to lot and that purity is impossible to establish when the constituents of the vaccine have never been defined. More than half the lots failed this supplemental testing. The Defense Department's answer was to exempt nine lots, even though they were produced under the same deficient conditions. Although the vaccine manufacturing facility closed in the fall of 1998, the Defense Department didn't admit until April 29, 1999, that the testing in the spring of 1998 was not done correctly. Shots continued, but no new vaccine was produced. One can only imagine how glossed over this point of the review was. BioPort was allowed to test for itself the quality, potency, and sterility of the vaccine. Only the results of those tests were reviewed by an outside entity.

3. *Implementation of an improved system to fully track vaccinations.* Tracking to ensure that the shot protocol was followed failed miserably. Even the secretary of defense got his fourth shot three weeks early. Noncompliance

percentages by mid-1999 were 88 percent for the Naval Reserve, 72 percent for the Marine Corps Reserve, 63 percent for the Army Reserve, 58 percent for the Army Guard, 33 percent for the Air Force Reserve, and 27 percent for the Air National Guard. Many Guard and Reserve members missed scheduled shots by weeks or months. In September 1999, the CANG was in 90 percent noncompliance. The GAO called this aspect insufficient.

4. *Approval of operational plans to administer the vaccinations and of communication plans by each military service branch to inform its personnel of the overall program.* Even Burrow felt strongly that this was a failure, based on the reactions of service members. Information from the Defense Department was full of half-truths and misrepresentations, both inadequate and misleading. Often, service members were not advised on how to submit a VAERS form. VAERS tracking was inadequate. Hardly any attempt was made to track adverse reactions in this passive program. Vaccine waivers and adverse-event reporting were not clear and were not being followed. The AVIP protocol was not consistent or properly applied.

The Four-Point Review was another sham and, by all standards of accountability, an attempt to whitewash a grave situation. With each item done in token fashion, the AVIP continued anyway. This failure alone should have been justification to end the AVIP immediately. The Defense Department's execution of the Four-Point Review was a failure.

Deception Extraordinaire

As if all of the aforementioned deceptions were not enough, consider some of these outrageous untruths and half-truths that the Defense Department published and used to promote the shot in order to entice members to roll up their sleeves.

1. Veterinarians have been using this vaccine for decades.
2. Thousands have taken this shot.
3. This shot is licensed since the 1950s.
4. Only one pilot has refused.
5. It's completely safe, even for my children.
6. It will protect against all strains for inhalation anthrax.
7. The vaccine is needed for force protection.
8. This shot is FDA approved.
9. Inhalation anthrax is 100 percent fatal.
10. The vaccine has undergone supplemental testing and independent review by an expert.
11. Iraq admitted using biological weapons and used them against its own people.

Let's hope that truth in government is not a forgotten concept.

The Defense Department's Public Enemy #1: Ms. Information!

To push this program down the throats of unwilling victims required propaganda. The military complained in congressional hearings that it was fighting an information war. What it didn't realize was that truth was not on its side, and that was why it was losing. The military blamed its losing battle on "sensational stories," "erroneous data," and "misinformation" on the Internet. But guess where it posted its own version of "misinformation"? Right! On the Internet.

Missing the point, the military did not appreciate the fact that so-called misinformation initiated twelve hearings in the U.S. Congress on the AVIP. Without valid claims and medical evidence, those hearings would not have occurred. Research done at the grass roots earned such high-level recognition and serious, timely attention because it represented an immediate challenge to readiness and safety. Plus, the misinformation that the Defense Department complained about was primarily information that it was aware of in the beginning but tried to hide, or that was forgotten when the department went for the political, the expedient, and the convenient solution, rather than the right one. Much of the misinformation was from its documents, briefing slides, meeting minutes, and test results. Intelligent and educated service members could examine the Defense Department's very general and doubtful claims, note the lack of authentic sources, and compare counterclaims that cited sources, many times the Defense Department's own documents.

The Army AVIP agency exists solely for the promotion of the vaccine and for fighting the so-called misinformation war. The AVIP sales pitch is led by a general officer who is spending $74 million over a six-year period (FY99-FY05).[15] The military hired a two-star Army general, who no doubt could have been used better elsewhere, to serve as the "vaccine salesman." Millions of dollars have been spent by the Defense Department to have speakers visit bases with brochures and videotapes, to blur areas of contention, and to convince all, through overwhelming command and peer pressure. At several bases, a vaccination expert came in and spent the first forty-five minutes of a sixty-five-minute briefing explaining the value and benefits of flu, chicken pox, and measles vaccines, before ever saying the word "anthrax." Is that a propaganda machine or what? It became a game of salesmanship. When an audience member asked a question about the effectiveness of the anthrax vaccine against different strains of anthrax, it was obvious that the doctor knew little about anthrax and that he was unaware of different strains. The Defense Department's credibility sank to all-time lows, as hundreds in the audience began looking at each other in disbelief. The main issues should have been science, health, ethics, and law.

Brochures and videos produced by the military were full of half-truths and unsubstantiated claims. That must be taxpayer value for dollars spent in the Defense Department's mind, but frankly, they were a waste of money because they did not deal with the real issues. Check out the Defense Department's anthrax Web site, and you can see where some of your money went. Did the Defense Department really believe that a pretty Web site with all the newfangled bells and whistles would entice members to exchange common sense and truth for a counterfeit? Appealing graphics can't conceal truth and reality forever in the Information Age.

BioPort Buyout

In September 1998, BioPort purchased the manufacturing facility from the state of Michigan for $24 million.[16] Less than two weeks after the purchase, BioPort was awarded a $45 million sole-source contract to supply anthrax vaccine for the Pentagon.

Two former lab directors, Robert Myers and Robert van Ravenswaay, initially tried to buy the lab themselves by forming their own company but withdrew after Michigan State Representative Lingg Brewer called it a conflict of interest. Myers himself said on November 30, 1996, to the *Lansing State Journal* that he was not involved in trying to buy the institute. He said, "I am a state employee…this would be a conflict of interest."[17] Employees knew of the $130 million contract with the Defense Department as early as October 2, 1996, well before the purchase.[18]

Note what happened in 1997, before the purchase. On January 7, Myers and his partner filed articles of incorporation under the name MBPI, indicating 60,000 shares. One week later, P.A. 522 authorized the sale of the lab. On June 10, the MBPI Articles of Incorporation were modified to increase the number of shares from 60,000 to 1 million. On December 16, the Army announced plans to quickly vaccinate all 2.4 million troops.

Brewer explained to me how Myers and van Ravenswaay used confidential information, which they had access to as officials of the public MBPI, to win the bid in 1998. A letter from Myers to an undisclosed losing bidder confirms that he was familiar with the terms of at least two other bids, information not available to other bidders. The pair also solicited financing from at least one other bidder, a clear violation of nondisclosure requirements.[19] The value of the plant was anywhere from "nominal" to $10.5 million. Brewer accuses them of manipulating the purchase price to lower than fair value in their contract with KPMG Peat Marwick, which establishes the fair market value, by failing to acknowledge the federal government's interest in purchasing greater quantities of products. Brewer says the two had a hand in writing the report as state employees. Later, these two joined BioPort's team, who, unsurprisingly, happened to be the top bidder. This was announced on June 2, 1998. When the state of Michigan turned the lab over, wisdom certainly did not prevail. Van Ravenswaay and Myers had previously received warning letters from the FDA in 1995 and 1997 criticizing them for poor management practices and for letting the lab slip into total disrepair.

It would seem that Myers, now BioPort's chief scientific officer, also has trouble telling the truth. On March 6, 2001, in defending the company's manufacturing process, he said, "Now licensed for thirty years, with 2 million doses given in the last two and a half years alone, the vaccine is proven safe. In total, there have been thirteen safety studies of many different types involving 366,000 patients, and there is no pattern emerging that would call the vaccine's safety into question. Anthrax vaccine is also purer than the diphtheria and tetanus vaccines we give our children and is safe or safer than these and other vaccines we give to our children and take ourselves as adults."[20]

In a letter to the editor in the *Washington Post* on February 7, 2000, Myers claimed that the company would never release a product that is not safe and effective and said its high standards would ensure that in the future. Yet the company shipped 100 doses of quarantined vaccine to Canada for its soldiers, and the FDA had to issue a recall in August 2000 for another mislabeled lot.

BioPort immediately received extraordinary contractual relief, which raised the price of the shot, more than doubling the cost of each dose to $10.64 (from $4.36 per dose), and decreased the total amount of vaccine to be delivered to the Defense Department. The Defense Department was throwing money at the problem and trying to make it easier for BioPort because all the department's eggs were in one basket, with only one supplier/contractor for the vaccine.

In 1998, BioPort was purchased by Fuad El-Hibri, a Venezuelan-turned-German, who became a U.S. citizen just after the purchase. El-Hibri's citizenship was described as a done deal at purchase time but was still not finalized until six months after the purchase was approved. In 1990, El-Hibri, who is of Lebanese descent, helped facilitate the purchase of anthrax vaccine for Saudi Arabia. El-Hibri also made a fortune during the Gulf War while working with the British seller of the anthrax vaccine, Porton Products International.

Less than a month after El-Hibri took over the business from MBPI, BioPort landed a $29 million exclusive contract with the Defense Department to manufacture, test, bottle, and store the anthrax vaccine. BioPort is expected to produce $60 million worth of anthrax vaccine over the next five years. By August 2001, the Pentagon had injected BioPort with $126 million.

BioPort is the sole supplier of the vaccine to the military. Having sole suppliers is not usually wise or frugal, and not necessarily safe, but perhaps still ethical and legal, if that was all there was to consider. It seems that common sense would dictate an alternate source for a vaccine in a program that supposedly is so critical for force protection. European bidders for the purchase of BioPort were reportedly turned down because they were not American citizens. An Italian firm, Gruppo Marcucci, offered more money up front ($16.5 million versus $3.5 million cash up front, the second-highest bid) and was endorsed by the Defense Department. However, the state wanted to award the contract to a U.S. company, and federal law prohibits the sale of a sole supplier of the anthrax vaccine to a foreign firm. Despite all this, they chose El-Hibri. He got a sweet deal, and much of BioPort's debt carries no interest.

More to Crowe About

To help seal the deal, former chairman of the Joint Chiefs of Staff Admiral William Crowe, fresh through the Washington "revolving door," was placed on the board of directors. He was the owner of 22.5 percent of Intervac LLC, a parent-type company. With no personal investment in the company, he was given a 13 percent share of BioPort. A former top Pentagon official who requested to remain anonymous said, "If Crowe is involved in this, you know it's fishy. It looks like another payoff for his help to Clinton."[21] Crowe had endorsed Clinton on camera at a critical time in his first presidential bid, when his tenuous relationship with the military was being covered extensively in the press. The first prize for Crowe was an ambassadorship to the United Kingdom. Behind "Door Number 2" was the anthrax treasure, it seems.

No one knows who may have used their military contacts to gain jobs with the contractor or who is now advising on the AVIP and also owns stock in BioPort. To avoid even the appearance of impropriety, an immediate and full financial disclosure of all BioPort/Defense Department employees, civilian and military, especially those involved in the JVAP and the surgeon general's office for the last few years, would be appropriate.

According to Major Glenn MacDonald, USAR (Retired), author of *Greed and Guinea Pigs: Risking the Health of the U.S. Military*, Crowe was part of the crew that sold Saddam Hussein the deadly means to wage war with anthrax germs for use against Iran.[22] The Defense Department met with the final bidders, so favoritism on this BioPort bid served many purposes, most of which the American people were not privy to. Crowe met off-site from the Pentagon with Undersecretary of Defense for Acquisitions and Technology David Oliver, coincidentally a retired Navy two-star admiral, perhaps to seal the deal.

Throw Me the Money

A 1999 audit showed a net loss for BioPort of $8 million and an estimated $18.4 million loss by December 2000. However, that same audit shows that BioPort spent over $2 million on items that may have been questionable, in light of its financial condition. For example, it may not have been appropriate to spend $1.1 million on office remodeling and furniture, parking lots, road paving, office moves, and renovation, including $23,000 on the chief executive officer's furniture. Senior management set aside bonuses for 2000 of $1.28 million, 109 percent greater than the manager's base salary. Also listed were excessive travel costs, excessive severance pay, and unsubstantiated consulting costs. More money gets tossed into the black hole. Congressman Jones, who requested the study from the House Armed Services Committee, said, "The report paints a bleak picture of the financial integrity and security of the anthrax program's only vaccine producer."[23] After continued investments of more than $45 million, BioPort is still failing inspections.

You have now seen how the AVIP is untested, unsafe, unnecessary, unpopular, and unethical. The Defense Department has displayed its lack of ethics, enforcing and defending this program using more than questionable tactics. Yet, defying common sense and withstanding these indictments, the AVIP is still alive. Incredible! Is our government so tangled in red tape and so bound by special interests and personal political agendas that we can't sort through legal issues either. Let's look at what should be the final nail in the coffin.

CHAPTER 6

There Is No Defense

Justice will not be served until those who are unaffected are as outraged as those who are.

—Benjamin Franklin

Injustice anywhere is a threat to justice everywhere.

—Martin Luther King, Jr.

An Unlawful Vaccine

One individual's personal and political agenda represented a huge hurdle for us in the 163rd Fighter Squadron, and everyone opposed to the AVIP in its current form. It came from our home state of Indiana, from Congressman Steve Buyer, a Gulf War veteran, and his superior, General Blanck. Besides being a congressman, Buyer was also a lieutenant colonel in the Army Reserves who himself suffered from Gulf War illness.

He told me personally that he took the anthrax shot. (It is "sick" rationale, but perhaps human nature, that many of those who took the shot wanted others to take the anthrax shot just because they took it. Then, if everything said about its lack of safety and people's getting sick proved true and they got sick, they would have more company.) When I described how the AVIP was placing part-time fighter pilots who were also full-time commercial airline pilots in a difficult position—the equivalent of self-medicating for all practical purposes—he asked what symptoms were so serious. I said blackouts, dizziness, and memory loss were most disconcerting and not conducive to flying high-performance airplanes, either a fighter aircraft or a commercial airline.

Buyer chuckled and said, "Memory loss—we all have memory loss from the shot. We joke about it." My jaw dropped! Seeing my shock, he repeated, "Yeah, we all joke about it." After regaining my composure, I went on to explain the dangers of those symptoms in the cockpit, still in wonderment that he didn't seem to get it.

We considered Buyer a key House member because he was chairman of the Personnel Subcommittee of the House Armed Services Committee. Any support from him, along with his Republican allies on the HGRC, would go a long way toward making progress on this issue for the good of his fellow troops and mine. Having been in the Army Reserves, he had inexplicable loyalties to Blanck that seemed to go even beyond a common military branch. The congressman later explained his praise for the general who had done so much for Gulf War victims.

While chairing a subcommittee hearing in October 2000, Buyer blasted off in an emotional tirade berating pilots because "they are the most pampered in the world, and if they didn't get their air conditioning and their pizza delivered on time, they complained (during the war), along with their hot showers."[1] One would not expect that lack of compassion or petty jealousy from someone who was suffering from Gulf War illness, especially the chair of the Personnel Subcommittee. We expected him to be more concerned with the health and welfare of the troops, plus the morale, readiness, and retention of highly trained and qualified personnel. In his congressional district, Grissom Air Force Base was estimated to lose at least 25 percent of its pilots. The weekend following his outburst, with no immediate hope to be found in Washington, twenty-eight aircrew and thirty-two additional support personnel from the Memphis, Tennessee, Air National Guard refused to be inoculated and submitted resignations or transfer requests. Dozens of pilots were lost from Buyer's own state.

The troops were not well served by either of these two men. Blanck, serving as committee chairman and no doubt using his power as Army surgeon general, allowed the Gulf War–illness investigation and information to be controlled favorable to Defense Department purposes, in the interests of a continued AVIP. Perhaps a follow-on career opportunity like Crowe's awaited both these men in retirement. Congressman Buyer evidently had plans to continue his military career or to benefit from that relationship rather than stand up for the troops, too, it seems. Let me explain.

In a statement before the House Committee on Veterans Affairs on November 16, 1999, Buyer acknowledged that the anthrax vaccine is not licensed for inhalation exposure. This makes the vaccine "investigational" under the Food, Drug, and Cosmetic Act. Buyer's endorsement of this policy represents a willful violation of federal law (10 USC 1107), which requires informed consent or a presidential waiver of informed consent to use investigational drugs or vaccines on military service members. He also implied that he was directly involved in the decision to use the anthrax vaccine, despite its not being licensed for the Defense Department's intended purpose. Buyer blocked legislation in the 106th Congress (HR 2343 and HR2348) that would have halted the anthrax vaccine program or made it voluntary. To clarify, Buyer said, "If the anthrax is actually placed on your skin, then it is FDA approved. If it is airborne through air assault, it is not FDA approved....It is FDA approved for one type but not for the other. But as a soldier, if I am going into the theater and I know they are going to drop anthrax on me, give me the vaccine. You know, give me the vaccine. And there is the pain that we have all endured in those judgments. Would you concur with what I have said?"[2]

No, I would not concur. Actually I wish I had been there to respond to that simple-minded question and naive understanding of this issue. Fine, if he would like to take the shot, and the same for many fine soldiers with him. But the critical issue is the forcing of anyone else to take what he publicly acknowledges is experimental, or investigational, and a violation of law. We have laws that protect us from people with other motives making that decision, the decision of what to inject into our bodies, for us. By law, "investigational" or "experimental" requires informed consent.

Buyer was asked, "[The shot] is not being used for its intended purpose?"

"That's correct," he answered.

"Its use is, then, off-label, investigational, and actually experimental for protection against inhalation anthrax."

"Well, uh—well, yes, that would be a fair assessment," said Buyer.

"Then, in accordance with the Nuremburg Code, the troops must have informed consent, right?"

"Yeah, I guess so," said Buyer.

"Then why don't we?" the question came, with no answer.[3]

Perhaps the memory loss caused by the shot that Buyer told me about at our first meeting was also affecting his judgment. That would not be the first time. Several months after our first meeting, I had the opportunity to confront Buyer at a town meeting in small-town Indiana. He fielded a question about the anthrax vaccine from the floor from a Fort Wayne pilot, Major Jeff Traver. Later, Traver and I talked privately with the congressman. Now he denied ever saying in Washington that his memory loss was from the shot. I believe he had forgotten once again. He might also have forgotten that I had a witness who heard that initial conversation and his response. I didn't forget. (Remember, I didn't take the shot.)

Another thing I didn't forget was the outstanding ethics and honor training that I received as an undergraduate student and cadet at the Air Force Academy, where we discussed scenarios of legal versus illegal orders. I remember driving my roommate nuts with statements like "It's all relative." I would make that statement when I became frustrated that there were so many personal standards of right and wrong and that people would use anything rather than an absolute standard to justify their behavior. When people are allowed to pick their own standards cafeteria-style, right and wrong is all relative to the individual's standards and to the situation-situation ethics. That's valid unless, of course, we believe in and adopt a common standard.

For military officers, that standard is the Constitution of the United States. And we take an oath of office that says we "will support and defend" that Constitution "against all enemies, foreign and domestic." And we "will obey the legal orders of those appointed over us." The rule of law is our guiding standard.

Applied to the AVIP, that meant three things to me: (1) I will defend the rights of my troops as defined by laws and by our Constitution and the basic human rights all people are entitled to; (2) Whatever enemy and motivation lies at the core of this AVIP is very destructive to trust, health, morale, combat readiness, and the efficiency of our military, and I will fight what is destroying those vital components; and (3) I have an obligation and the command responsibility, in addition to the legal responsibility, to understand orders and their implications and to determine or investigate their lawfulness, especially when they clearly contradict current laws and ethics. From the letter and intent of 10 USC 1107, 21 USC 355, Presidential Executive Order 13139, and Defense Department regulation 6200.2, the order to take the anthrax vaccine is an illegal order because informed consent is not provided. Bills from the House and Senate, HR106-556 and SR-103-97, respectively, also support this view.

With the alarming and overwhelming mountain of evidence against it, AVIP is completely indefensible in its current form. There is no justification or rationale for continuing this program. At the same time, we the people are left defenseless. If the time and energy spent in covering up the issues had been focused instead on creating an effective vaccine, we might now have a solution that provided real defense for the military and for the public.

Courts-martial in the United States that resulted from the AVIP did not even allow the question of the legal status of the order to be examined. The only justification that the Defense Department offers is that it is an order given from a superior officer. Therefore, it is legal. However, there is much more to consider, like basic rights and freedoms.

In March 1998, Mike Kipling, 45, was stationed in Kuwait City among 400 Canadian soldiers who were to be given the anthrax vaccine. Kipling, a sergeant from Winnipeg, Canada, refused the vaccine. Canada conducted a court-martial of Kipling, who was charged with failing to obey an order to be inoculated with the anthrax vaccine. Testimony revealed that potency varied by as much as forty times among different packages of the shot, and the shot caused long-term side effects in at least 30 percent of soldiers who received it. The vaccine they were given had expired in 1993, but individual vaccines were relabeled and given in 1998. In the end, the Canadian Charter of Rights and Freedoms was upheld by Canada's top military judge, and he upheld Kipling's right to refuse the vaccine.

The Law and Experimentation

On October 15, 1996, the Army advertised in the *Washington Post* for "experimental" subjects for anthrax research related to the manufacturer's new IND (Investigational New Drug) status. "Very intriguing!" as *ABC News* reporter Nicholas Regush would say.[4] Notice also that BioPort did not put the ad in, nor did any scientific body for research. The Army placed the ad, and testing was completed a couple years later. "Our testing is done. It's safe and effective!" That was quick. And who did the research? Are we to believe that they are not doing research now on their own captive human guinea pigs, the troops? That would not be a stretch to believe, considering the context of the AVIP. What about another context?

At the height of the anthrax terror attacks, the CDC acquired 220,000 doses from the Pentagon for 1,000 lab workers and field investigators most likely to come in contact with anthrax. How many were truly ready to instantly make this potentially life-changing decision? When anthrax exposure occurred at American Media, Inc. in Florida, more than 1,000 were offered the shot, and only one person accepted. A few days later, one more person said he'd be willing to take the shot.

News reports describe postal workers facing the same shot decision. According to the *Washington Post*, at the beginning of 2002, only about four-dozen of an estimated 6,000 workers in New Jersey and Washington, D.C., chose to risk taking the shot, despite a very real and deadly threat. From this particular anthrax attack, eleven got inhalation anthrax and five died. Seven got the cutaneous form. New fears are that deadly anthrax spores can live in the lungs for up to 100 days. Many are now struggling with the decision to take the shot to help fight chances of infection, because these dormant spores may reactivate even after the sixty days of antibiotics many have already taken. The responses of the Department of Health and Human Services (HHS) and the CDC to recent bioterrorism attacks constitute violations of medical ethics. They "made the still unlicensed [anthrax] vaccine available to potentially exposed postal workers and congressional staffers not as an immunization, but as a treatment supplemental to antibiotics—without a scintilla of scientific evidence that such inoculations could help prevent the disease in exposed individuals. Even the HHS and CDC officials responsible refused to recommend that the workers actually take the shots."[5]

Many making this decision are ill-informed about the vaccine. HHS Secretary Tommy Thompson limited the vaccine available to 3,000 in Washington, D.C., New Jersey, New York, Connecticut, and Florida. Officials now believe that exposures were to a much higher level than previously known. Government physicians say that up to 3,000 times the lethal dose may have been inhaled by some workers who were exposed. News reports called the shot "experimental" for the American public. And, civilians who chose to take the shot were required to sign a waiver, a five-page informed-consent form showing the risks and benefits of the shot and to acknowledge that informed consent was given.

There was no parallel to this in the military, no informed-consent process. Why is there a double standard for experimentation on the military, especially in peacetime? The government justifies the already unlawful situation with a semantics sidestep: for the military, it's called "pre-exposure treatment"; for civilians, it's called "post-exposure experimental treatment."

Many physicians agree with the Defense Department's own status of the vaccine as being experimental. On April 1, 1999, the Association of American Physicians and Surgeons submitted in its report to the HGRC the following: "Informed consent must be observed even by the military. No consent can be informed if the information is based on science that violates fundamental precepts of honesty and integrity and lacks a proper research design that can disprove the hypothesis of safety, if indeed there are significant adverse effects."[6] History, ethics, and the legal use of medicine combine to protect us today and to provide standards like informed consent.

Article 5 of the Washington Treaty of 1922, the Geneva Protocols, and the Hague Conventions all protect us and provide an international-law foundation for rejecting chemical and biological warfare. But practices in the Gulf War and acceptance of a different standard for the Defense Department's relationship with the FDA may signal a significant and dangerous shift taking place and may represent violations of standards from Nuremburg that we previously embraced.

The Nuremburg Code

The Nuremburg Code originated from the trial of twenty-three Nazi doctors and scientists at Nuremberg in 1947. Karl Brandt and others in the Nazi high command were accused of war crimes and crimes against humanity. Seven were hanged. U.S. judges acting under the authority of the U.S. Army were charged with protecting basic laws of humanity. Excerpts of the code follow:

> The voluntary consent of the human subject is absolutely essential to exercise free power of choice, without the intervention of any element of force, fraud, deceit, duress, over-reaching or other ulterior form of constraint or coercions; and should have sufficient knowledge and comprehension of the element of the subject matter involved as to enable him to make an understanding and enlightened decision.
>
> The experiment should be so designed and based on the results of animal experimentation and a knowledge of the natural history of the disease or other problem under study and the anticipated results will justify the performance of the experiment.
>
> Experiments should be so conducted as to avoid all unnecessary physical and mental suffering and injury. No experiment should be so conducted where there is a priori reason to believe that death or disabling injury will occur. During the course of the experiment the human subject should be at liberty to bring the experiment to an end if he has reached the physical or mental state where the continuation of the experiment seems to him to be impossible.

The Nuremburg Code has been codified as an integral part of U.S. domestic law and international law. The AVIP should not only stand up in the world court of legal opinion, where people are not under the heavy-handedness and intimidation of the U.S. military, but should also demonstrate that the United States remains a world leader on human rights issues.

The FDA granted what are called Rule 23(d) waivers for the use of two agents in the Gulf War. One was pyridostigmine bromide, a nerve gas pretreatment, and the other was an agent to protect against botulism. Rule 23(d) allows for direct violations of the Nuremberg Code, but what a horrible precedent and hypocritical example we demonstrate internationally. Members of the military, unlike civilians, do not have the right to refuse medical "treatment" that can make them fit for duty or return them to active duty. The stretch is that Rule 23(d) did not apply to anthrax, nor does the term "treatment" equate to "pretreatment," as the

Defense Department is using anthrax vaccines to be prepared preemptively for a biological warfare attack.

The relationship between the Defense Department and the FDA leaves much to be desired when it comes to safety and integrity in the JVAP. A previous Memorandum of Understanding (MOU) dates back to 1974. On May 21, 1987, the FDA entered the current MOU with the Defense Department, which applies today. This MOU established procedures to be followed by the Defense Department and the FDA regarding the investigational use of drugs, biologics, and medical devices. It addressed the possibility of a need for expedited review of an IND by the FDA to meet Defense Department requirements concerning national defense. However, this agreement "does not allow the DOD to perform research on humans without submitting an IND [application], and it requires the DOD to comply with all FDA regulations."[7]

Minutes from the U.S. Army institutional review board meeting at Fort Detrick show that in October 1990, the board recognized that "the ability to use investigational drugs, biological [sic] and devices in human subjects is predicated on a subject's ability to trust that health care professionals are working in his best interest."[8] The context of this discussion was an explanation for why the board voted to require informed consent to the botulism vaccine before using it in combat.

This represents a sea change in philosophy compared with ten years ago. Back then, informed consent was provided for, even in war—a novel and upstanding concept, compared with the philosophy of today's AVIP. Perhaps the Defense Department has realized that with the erosion or complete meltdown in a subject's "ability to trust," it faces an entirely different situation today. But to not provide for informed consent in peacetime is a quantum leap, and an unlawful one. Or could it be that now the Defense Department realizes that the troops know this medical treatment is not in their "best interest"? Those are certainly factors. But it might be the third aspect of that phrase from the minutes, "health care professionals," that overrules the thinking ten years ago. True professionals do not act outside of legal and ethical principles.

By offering informed consent, consistent with its meeting minutes of ten years ago, the Defense Department could stay within the boundaries of the Nuremburg Code. As George Annas wrote in the *New England Journal of Medicine*, "The United States is and should remain at the forefront of the worldwide human rights movement. In crafting exceptions for the military, even in wartime, we do more damage to ourselves than to our enemies because any major retreat from supporting human rights is destructive both to our credibility and to the cause of human rights."[9] That's exactly why our example of protecting human rights at home is so important.

The Defense Department should have asked the FDA to rescind Rule 23(d).

Despite a petition to the FDA, the Defense Department supported keeping the waiver in place. Evidently, either the department felt that not every soldier is intelligent or capable enough of making a decision on informed consent, or the department is lazy and realizes that it will take effort on the battlefield to comply with the Nuremburg Code. The volunteer force is so conveniently available that they have become prisoners of their own Army, human subjects for its medical experiments. How's that for a nation leading the way on human rights?

The Fourth Amendment

The Fourth Amendment to the Constitution protects Americans' rights to privacy. Invasion by unwanted chemicals and contaminants into the bloodstream that may cause bodily damage can be assumed by the reasonable man for common-law purposes to be protected under this amendment. Certain rights are inalienable, and we all value enjoyment of life, liberty, and the pursuit of happiness. As Brigadier General Busbee said, "Soldiers have the same Constitutional rights as other citizens." Now, if we could get our actions in line with our words and our beliefs, we might make some moral and legal progress with respect to the AVIP.

The Fifth Amendment

"No person shall ... be deprived of life, liberty, or property, without due process of law." Vaccinating citizens with a hazardous drug without their informed consent as required by law and launching a full-scale cover-up when the truth about their illnesses was evident is a violation of this amendment. The Declaration of Independence emphasized, "We hold these Truths to be self-evident, that all Men are created equal, that they are endowed by their Creator with certain unalienable Rights, that among these are Life, Liberty, and the Pursuit of Happiness."

On the Books Now

Current U.S. statutory law requires that informed consent be obtained for all investigational use of drugs. In 1990, after Iraq's invasion of Kuwait, the Defense Department sought a waiver of the informed-consent requirements of existing human experimentation regulations from the FDA. With this waiver, the Defense Department could authorize military use of investigational drugs and vaccines on soldiers involved in the Gulf War without their informed consent. The waiver was granted on the basis of military expediency. Even though "...in all peacetime applications we strongly believe in informed consent and ethical foundations,"[10] this is not true with AVIP.

The FDA granted the request and issued a new general regulation permitting drug-waiver approval on the basis that consent is not feasible in a specific military operation involving combat or the immediate threat of combat. The FDA granted the waiver for only two agents. Anthrax was not included.

Principles are codified in 50 U.S. Code 1520a, which prevents the Defense Department from conducting mass-scale experiments. The mandatory AVIP violates 10 U.S. Code 1107, Executive Order 13139, and Defense Department Directive 6200.2. The secretary of defense may not conduct any test or experiment involving the use of chemical or biological agents on human subjects. He may do so if he has received informed consent under certain conditions.

After lessons learned from the Gulf War, both HR 106-556 and SR 103-97 called the use of the anthrax vaccine experimental and investigational. Unfortunately these resolutions were not passed.

Executive Order 13139, signed by former President Clinton on October 22, 1999, allows the president to waive informed consent under emergency or wartime conditions for the military, but only when absolutely necessary. Title 10, Section 1107, of the U.S. Code states that waivers for informed consent when using investigational drugs may be granted only if the president determines in writing that obtaining consent is not feasible, that it is contrary to the best interests of the member, or that it is not in the interests of national security.

Headlines from the October 22, 1999, *Insight Magazine* read: "Clinton Orders Human Experiments."[11] The intent of this order was to protect service members from receiving experimental vaccines not approved by the FDA. Some members of Congress who were already aware of the failings of the AVIP saw this order as the president's attempt to cover up Defense Department violations of FDA protocol.

Recent Cases

Two U.S. Air Force Reserve lawyers (JAGs), Lieutenant Colonel John Michels Jr., a 1977 USAFA graduate and pilot, and Major Bruce Smith, wrote a legal memorandum. The memo stated that it is illegal for the U.S. military to order service members to submit to the anthrax vaccine because the program is inconsistent with federal law. They drafted the memo when serving on the legal team defending Major Bates from Dover Air Force Base. They also described how Air Force Instruction 40-403, entitled "Clinical Investigations in Medical Research Guidance and Procedures," provides protection for service members. It "very explicitly spells out the right of Air Force personnel to receive detailed information about the possible side effects of all investigational drugs and therapies, and specifies that each member must then give his or her consent in writing before being subjected to any regimen."[12]

They successfully defended Bates and kept him from being imprisoned, when he was facing a potential five years in prison. Bates was threatened with a court-martial when he refused to take the shot while on active duty, after fourteen years and 3,200 flying hours. He was given a "general" discharge, which is below an honorable discharge status. He was also fined $3,200, plus another $6,000 payroll penalty. Without the mounting public and congressional pressure when he refused the order to take the shot, the penalty may have been stiffer. As described in chapter 2, when a minimum of fifteen people became sick in his squadron at Dover Air Force Base, Bates refused to risk hardship for his family. He has an autistic child that requires extra attention at home, which a sick or injured father may not be able to provide. Bates also had a doctor's written opinion stating that he would be susceptible to illness because of his family medical history if he took the shot. Medical records later showed that more than a hundred service members at Dover reported that the vaccine made them ill.

In another serious court challenge, Attorney General Richard Blumenthal of Connecticut has charged that it is illegal to mandate the AVIP, which uses experimental drugs, for National Guard troops, because they are assets of the state. He openly charged that the military is forcing its people to serve as guinea pigs. This twist proves interesting, as it rallies the debate of power separation between state and federal responsibilities and roles. Because the Defense Department has proven resistant to taking prudent medical care or picking up the costs and assuming liability for Guard troops, which are assets belonging to each state's governor, they have less standing under the federally mandated AVIP. A proposed bill that prevents the federal government from using experimental drugs on the state's National Guard troops passed the General Assembly's public safety committee and was forwarded to the public health committee in Connecticut. Along with Massachusetts, Connecticut is pursuing legislation to protect its state employees from illegal abuse.

In Blumenthal's recent letter to Secretary of Defense Rumsfeld, he reminded him that (1) anthrax vaccine has not been proved safe and effective for its intended use in that the AVA has never been licensed for protection against inhalation anthrax; (2) the vaccine is not being manufactured in accordance with either its site license or product license; (3) the vaccine is not being administered according to the license; and (4) since the anthrax vaccine has not been tested on humans, there is no basis for concluding that its use is safe and effective for prevention of inhaled anthrax.[13]

Without testing on humans, the anthrax vaccine can never advance beyond the stage of an investigational drug. In August 1992, two Army physicians wrote an article in *Military Medicine* claiming that biowarfare vaccines are always experimental. William Raub, Ph.D., deputy assistant secretary for science policy at HHS, stated in his November 9, 1999, testimony that new regulations were needed to provide for investigational drugs to be tested ethically on humans.[14] The testing would be so deadly that human trials are not ethical.

Consider then the Defense Department's consistent pattern and handling of the Tick-Borne Encephalitis (TBE) vaccine program. The FDA determined in an October 1997 PAC special report that the Defense Department's use of the TBE vaccine during Operations Joint Endeavor/Joint Guard violated federal regulations pertaining to investigational products on several accounts. These included "record-keeping failures, failure to monitor fully the study's progress, failure to ensure that protocol was followed so safety and efficacy can be assessed, promotion of safety and efficacy for the investigational product, and failure to obtain Institutional Review Board approval of informed-consent documents."[15] This pattern was clearly identified by the Rockefeller Report years earlier.

The Rockefeller Report

The 1994 Rockefeller Report[16] examined biological experimentation on the U.S. military. Veterans believe that from 1945 until 1962, they were used as guinea pigs in numerous nuclear detonation tests. "Volunteer" soldiers were given hallucinogenic drugs (LSD, for one) in the 1950s by the Defense Department working with the Central Intelligence Agency (CIA). These studies were kept secret until the mid-1970s. Actions in the Gulf War furthered the Defense Department's purposes of illegal experimentation. The investigation and report concludes that the anthrax vaccine is not proven safe and effective as used in the Persian Gulf. It says that "off-label" use, using the vaccine for a purpose not originally intended, should be considered investigational when it is used as a protection against biological warfare.

The report contains survey results of 150 Gulf War veterans (120 male, 30 female). The survey shows that:

■ 136 (91 percent) were ill since returning from the Gulf.
■ 75 (50 percent) identified at least one investigational drug they took in the Gulf.
■ 25 (17 percent) received an unidentified vaccination.
■ 128 (85 percent) received no information after the Gulf War from the Defense Department or the Veterans Administration (VA) concerning investigational drugs.
■ 68 (45 percent) received the anthrax vaccine.
  Within this 45 percent:
  • 31 (46 percent) received one vaccination.
  • 31 (46 percent) received two vaccinations.
  • 2 (3 percent) received three vaccinations.
  • 2 (6 percent) received an unknown number.
  • 61 (90 percent) received no oral or written information about the shot.
  • 58 (85 percent) were told they could not refuse it.
  • 29 (43 percent) experienced immediate side effects.
  Of the 16 women receiving the shot:
  • 12 (75 percent) received no warning of risk if pregnant.

Findings and conclusions of the Rockefeller Report include:

1. For at least fifty years, the Defense Department has intentionally exposed military personnel to potentially dangerous substances, often in secret.
2. The Defense Department has repeatedly failed to comply with required ethical standards when using human subjects in military research during war or threat of war.
3. The Defense Department incorrectly claims that because its goal was treatment, the use of investigational drugs in the Persian Gulf Wars was not research.
4. The Defense Department used investigational drugs in the Persian Gulf War in ways that were not effective.
5. Records of anthrax vaccinations are not suitable to evaluate safety.
6. The Defense Department and the VA have repeatedly failed to provide information and medical follow-up to those who participated in military research or to those who were ordered to take investigational drugs.
7. The Federal government has failed to support scientific studies that provide information about the reproductive problems experienced by veterans who were intentionally exposed to potentially dangerous substances.
8. The Federal Government has failed to support scientific studies that provide timely information for compensation decisions regarding military personnel who were harmed by various exposures.
9. Participation in military research is rarely included in military medical records, making it impossible to support veterans' claims for service-connected disabilities from military research.
10. The Defense Department has demonstrated a pattern of misrepresenting the dangers of various military exposures, a pattern that continues today.

The Defense Department continues to duck responsibility, accountability, and mandatory reform. Worst of all, it ducks any attempts to end AVIP.

Some of the recommendations made in the Rockefeller Report are that (1) Congress should deny the Defense Department request for a blanket waiver to use investigational drugs in case of war or threat of war; (2) the FDA should reject any applications from the Defense Department that do not include data on women and long-term follow-up data; and (3) the Feres Doctrine should not be applied for military personnel who are harmed by inappropriate human experimentation when informed consent has not been given.[17]

The Feres Doctrine

The military legal system provides sovereign and official immunity to government officials in their decisions and programs when conducting official government business. The doctrine prevents the abuse of human and constitutional rights from being challenged in the federal judiciary. This blank check allows for "absolute power to corrupt absolutely" and allows programs like the AVIP to go relatively unchecked for long periods. Commanders bask in their unfettered authority, enjoying the excess privileges of power and, all too often, the opportunity to abuse. Meanwhile, victims without recourse pay with their health and financial security, many times for a lifetime. During the 1990s, the White House promoted a dangerous attitude that leadership was above the law. The Feres Doctrine encourages further abuse with a license to act under cover of official government business. The implication of the AVIP for service members is that officials may as well roll up service members' sleeves, vaccinate their arms, inject the poison, tie their hands, bend them over, kiss their legal rights goodbye, and destroy their health and lives.

Who Is Regulating the Regulators?

In March 1990, Army doctors described the anthrax vaccine as an "unlicensed experimental vaccine." In an article titled "Military Immunizations," Colonel (Dr.) Ernest Takafuji of the Army Surgeon General's Office and Colonel (Dr.) Philip Russell of Fort Detrick described anthrax as a limited-use vaccine. Because the vaccine is, by their own admission, "unlicensed" and "experimental" and a "limited-use vaccine," clearly the AVIP is using it for purposes other than its original intent. Under FDA rules, its use requires that informed consent be obtained from all shot recipients.

Furthermore, as shown in an Army/Science Applications International Corporation (SAIC) briefing slide dated October 19,1995, the legal status of the anthrax vaccine was clearly identified when the Defense Department was planning to submit its application to get the vaccine approved for inhalation anthrax. The department clearly recognized that a substantial informed-consent obstacle existed unless scientific tests were developed to satisfy federal regulators, even under existing FDA regulations. The slide says, "This vaccine is not licensed for aerosol exposure expected in a biological warfare environment."[18]

To escape informed consent, the Pentagon chose a different approach than following the letter and intent of existing laws. The assistant secretary of defense for health affairs, Dr. Stephen Joseph, sought FDA permission to use the anthrax vaccine to protect U.S. troops against the threat of an Iraqi biological weapons attack. He said, "While the package insert for this vaccine is nonspecific as to the route of exposure, DOD has long interpreted the scope of the license to include inhalation anthrax." He wrote to FDA lead deputy commissioner Dr. Michael Friedman, "Please advise whether the FDA has any objection."[19]

Friedman's response is carefully worded. He remarks on the "paucity of data" regarding the effectiveness of anthrax vaccine protection versus inhalation anthrax, then states that the use of the vaccine for that purpose "is not inconsistent with the current label." First, he admits it has not been sufficiently tested. Then he compromises FDA standards with his opinion by not enforcing actual and specific label usage of the vaccine. He virtually says that because that particular off-label use for the vaccine, meaning "inhalation," is not specifically prohibited on the actual product label, it is not inconsistent with the label to use it that way. The problem with this huge twist in philosophy is that it gives the Defense Department free rein. This response paints the picture of FDA officials turning their heads and looking the other way. As was pointed out in congressional testimony, using the vaccine for inhalation anthrax is also inconsistent with the label. That's what "off-label" means—using a drug for a purpose it was not designed for. It is required, for any product, drug or otherwise, to list every approved use on the label. Uses not listed are not consistent with its purpose and are considered "off-label," which requires informed consent.

The Defense Department used this letter of personal opinion to further its cause with the mandatory AVIP. Blumenthal reminded Rumsfeld that with Friedman's short letter of personal opinion and one stroke of the pen, Friedman had effectively wiped out ten years of Defense Department analysis and twenty-five years of FDA law protecting the safety and well-being of our citizens.

The Defense Department uses that March 13, 1997, letter from Friedman as justification for utilizing the vaccine against inhalation exposure. Apparently, the department is unaware or ignorant of the fact that "a statement or advice given by an FDA employee orally, or given in writing, but not under this section or Sec. 10.90 is an informal communication that represents the best judgment of that employee at that time but does not constitute an advisory opinion, does not necessarily represent the formal position of FDA, and does not bind or otherwise obligate or commit the agency to the views expressed."[20] Laws and regulations are in place to protect citizens when people fail. DOD uses this opinion as "license to experiment."

In September 1995, SAIC contracted to develop an Army plan to obtain FDA approval for a license amendment to include aerosol anthrax exposure. The application identifies the correct legal status of the vaccine. The implied obstacle is informed consent, unless scientific tests were developed to satisfy federal regulatory requirements: "This vaccine is not licensed for aerosol exposure expected in a biological warfare environment."[21] The minutes of the Joint Program Office for Biological Defense meeting on October 20, 1995, show that the Army knew it needed a license to use the vaccination for inhalation anthrax, modifying the current license to allow for fewer injections and expanding the indication to include protection against aerosol challenge of spores.

A September 20, 1996, IND application with the FDA is still pending five and a half years later. Three reasons for this IND are a change in "indication" (purpose for use) to include inhalation anthrax, a change of dosage, and a change in route of administration. At first, Army medical leadership agreed that a change was needed to allow for informed consent; but it reversed positions within a month of Secretary of Defense Cohen's being confirmed as secretary of defense. Following that came pressure on the FDA by the Defense Department to give permission to begin using the vaccine for inhalation anthrax without a new license and without completing the scientific investigation proposed by the IND application.

Specifically, FDA Form 1571, which submits this application, lists "inhalation anthrax" as the only reason covered under this submission. So, one year later, in January 1999, the owner of BioPort acknowledged in the company's update to the FDA that the vaccine was not licensed for the purpose that the Defense Department was using it. The update to the application specifically mentions inhalation anthrax as the only indication and the only reason for submission.

Under 21 U.S.C. P321, the vaccine is properly considered an Investigational New Drug, because it is being used in a way inconsistent with the original licensing. The anthrax vaccine license was obtained for veterinary and agriculture settings for protection against cutaneous anthrax. Before the Gulf War, the largest batch was 7,500 doses. When defense officials all of a sudden needed 300,000 doses, and only 70,000 had been manufactured up to that time, changes were made to increase production. However, the FDA was never notified, as required by law. The vaccine was not intended for a mass inoculation to protect against inhalation anthrax.

The FDA has failed to approve use for inhalation anthrax three times, on December 15, 1997, on May 18, 1998, and on March 30, 1999. The Defense Department publicly insists that it applied only for a change of dosage and route of administration, contradicting the application form and its earlier statements. However, as late as June 30, 1999, El-Hibri, BioPort's president and chief executive officer, said that the company continues to hold an IND application (IND6847). He admits that the vaccine is investigational and that it requires informed consent.

In addition to all this legal mumbo jumbo, all the testing of the Brachman study was on the originally licensed vaccine, not on the changed vaccine that is being given to troops. Testing was not properly accomplished and documented on the vaccine now being given, so common sense dictates that military troops have become test subjects with the new vaccine and that they are part of the Defense Department's larger JVAP experiment.

Adulteration

"A drug shall be deemed adulterated if it has been prepared, packed, or held under unsanitary conditions whereby it may have been contaminated with filth, or whether it may have been rendered injurious to health; or if it is a drug and the methods used in, or the facilities or controls for, its manufacture, processing, packing or holding do not conform to or are not operated or administered in conformity with current good manufacturing practice."[22]

Before distributing a product made using a change, an applicant shall demonstrate through appropriate validation and/or other clinical and/or nonclinical laboratory studies, all considerations of adverse effect of the change on the identity, strength, quality, purity or potency of the product as they may relate to the safety or effectiveness of the product.[23]

New fermenters were added in 1990, and that is considered a major change. An amendment was finally approved in July 1993, nearly two and a half years later. Meanwhile, BioPort was producing and distributing without the FDA approval required. Along with new fermenters came new filters. These new filters also constitute a major change. Potency increased a hundredfold because of this change. In February 1998, the FDA noted in its inspection that prior to August 1997, the filters were not validated nor were they integrity tested. "This filter is the only sterile filtration step in the manufacturing process."[24] And we wondered why people were getting sick from this shot. Now, not much is left to the imagination.

According to GAO supervisor Sushil Sharma, who helped investigate those changes, the FDA knew about the changes long ago. The FDA allowed service members to be inoculated with an "adulterated product"—a clinical term for a product not fit for human consumption. The FDA allowed violations that would normally result in serious civil or criminal penalties, and seems to have turned a blind eye in its oversight and surveillance of the BioPort anthrax production facility. The result was that every dose delivered after the 1990 manufacturing change was done without a proper licensing amendment.

In 1997, MBPI relabeled 1.5 million doses; they soaked off the labels, then relabeled them with new expiration dates. No stability testing program was in place at the time, so the vaccine may have destabilized and disintegrated over time. No procedures for removing and relabeling filled vials of vaccine were in effect. No procedure was in effect for reconciling the vials with the original lot once the labels were removed; therefore, the vials could not be reidentified correctly with the original labels. Incorrect lot numbers means misbranding. The MBPI also redated bulk vaccine that had expired without justification or approved procedures, which means it is an adulterated drug. These practices required a supplement to the product license, which was not sought or approved at the time of these events. CGMP requires compliance; otherwise, by FDA definition, the result is an adulterated product. Use of adulterated and misbranded drugs is prohibited under U.S. Code 331.

Referring to Sections 501(a)(2)(b) of the FDC Act, Sammie Young, CBER/CDER compliance deputy director, commented that the FDA is condoning the use of adulterated anthrax vaccine in government employees.[25] On December 15, 2001, Zoon said, "[The vaccine] would not be licensed as safe and effective."[26] This vaccine is being offered to civilians and is being treated as an experimental vaccine that requires informed consent, and it is perplexing that the military is not afforded the same legal protection.

Dr. Anthony Fauci, a retired colonel, USAFR (Medical Service Corps), is the director of the National Institute of Health. He is an FDA regulating official with years of experience in the drug-approval process. According to Fauci, "We have come a long way since Nuremburg and the Helsinki agreement in dealing with experimentation involving human subjects; we should not take a giant step backward [with respect to the recent anthrax terror attacks]. CDC employees and/or U.S. postal service personnel should not be treated as human guinea pigs in this post-Nuremburg era."[27]

Zoon was questioned about how aboveboard the government is going to be. She said, "These lots would never meet the criteria for release for licensure."[28]

Why, unless we have a double standard here, is the vaccine dubbed "licensed for military use"?

She went on, "And the only reason that these would be considered, as I said, was [in] an emergency situation with full informed consent in the nature of this product and what the deviations were ... making sure that was transparent so the individual looking at this could be fully informed."[29]

Young then asked her, "Will the informed-consent statement say to the people from CDC that your product is legally adulterated?"

She responded, "I think it would lay out the manufacturing deviations. It would also lay out where it didn't meet spec."[30]

Talk about spin! Have they forgotten the abuse of discretion involved in the release of the live polio vaccine in the United States thirty years ago? This shot opened the government to millions of dollars in tort liability claims.

Also consider what aspects of the vaccine make it a new drug. When a new application for a drug arises, or its method of administration is modified, or when dosage or duration changes, you have a new drug. For the first twenty years, the anthrax vaccine was used on military researchers and test animals but only on a very limited population. Now it is being used for a mass immunization program. Its use from 1990 to the present for anything other than what is prescribed, recommended, or suggested in the labeling makes this a new drug, an unlicensed, unproven drug.

Any drug used for a purpose other than its original intent under its approved FDA license is an investigational drug and requires informed consent. The anthrax vaccine is definitely being used to prevent inhalation anthrax, and it was designed only for cutaneous anthrax exposure such as what wool-sorters and veterinarians may experience. It was not designed for mass inoculation of troops to prevent inhalation anthrax. And it doesn't take a lawyer or a doctor to figure that out. The approved labeling says that the vaccine is recommended only for individuals who come in contact with animal products; persons at high risk, such as veterinarians and others handling potentially infected animals; and persons involved in biological investigational activities.[31]

Lawful Orders

The *Manual for Courts-Martial* states: "The order must relate to military duty, which includes all activities reasonably necessary to accomplish a military mission, or safeguard or promote the morale, discipline, and usefulness of members of a command and directly connected with the maintenance of good order in the service. The order may not, without such a valid military purpose, interfere with private rights or personal affairs. However, the dictates of a person's conscience, religion, or personal philosophy cannot justify or excuse the disobedience of an otherwise lawful order."

The test case law comes from *The United States v. Flynn*, where the court said that among other things, an order cannot be contrary to established law or regulation. The vaccine is not the one that was originally approved by the FDA, so the order should be considered unlawful. On those grounds alone, the order violates FDA regulations. The legality of orders may be questioned, and it is the responsibility of the courts to determine the lawfulness of orders when issues are raised. The Defense Department and commander's paternalistic response that the order is legal because it comes from above does not settle the question of lawfulness that a court must determine.

Additionally, individual rights that are protected by the Constitution and statute are not subject to military orders, which are arbitrary and unreasonable. From *The United States v. Chadwell*, "Persons in the military service are neither puppets nor robots. They are not subject to the willynilly push or pull of a capricious superior.... In that area they are human beings endowed with legal and personal rights which are not subject to military order. Only the violation of a 'lawful order' was punishable by court-martial."

The soldier's duty is to obey lawful orders, but he or she may disobey, and in some circumstances, must disobey unlawful orders. While the accused can never be punished for failing to obey an unlawful order, liability cannot be escaped if unlawful orders are followed. When laws are violated, the defense of "following orders" melts away. If the accused knew or could have reasonably been expected to know that the order violated laws, he may be expected to also disobey the obvious unlawful order. "Military leaders remain responsible for insuring that the law of the land is carried out and are not permitted merely to accept the orders of an immediate superior when that order is known to conflict with national policy... [and the law of the land.]" [34] An order is unlawful if it violates the precepts of the Constitution or an act of Congress.

When applying ethical principles, the leader and the subordinate are equal. "The soldier cannot surrender ... his right to make ultimate moral judgments. He cannot deny himself as a moral individual ... As a soldier he owes obedience; as a man, he owes disobedience…. Only rarely will the military man be justified in following the dictates of private conscience against the dual demand of military obedience and state welfare."[33] Orders should enjoy the presumption and treatment status of being legal; commanders and superiors desiring good order and discipline should not have to worry about every order being questioned. However, when informed with evidence to the contrary, and when circumstance could determine life or death, officers have a legal obligation to investigate and, if warranted, to question the legality of the order.

Malham Wakin, a long-time philosophy instructor from the U.S. Air Force Academy, summarizes General John Ryan's 1972 policy letter to commanders: "It is clear that the ideal which General Ryan proposes places the value of integrity above unquestioning obedience of commands."[34]

Ryan wrote, "Integrity is the most important responsibility of command."[35] Integrity makes obedience and loyalty possible. Wakin further states, "It is no longer the case that extreme value is placed on personal loyalty to a commander [or loyalty to a program]; that aspect of military honor is transferred to the oath of office which requires allegiance to the Constitution and to the position rather than the person of the President as Commander-in-Chief."[36] As we were taught at the USAFA, good judgment is critical.

The Oath of an Officer

The first loyalty for a citizen soldier is to the Constitution. Our Oath of Office makes that clear, and the United States is governed by the rule of law. A military officer has an obligation to determine the lawfulness of orders before executing and obeying those orders. Most orders will not be questioned. However, the AVIP, replete with contradictions and violations of standing laws, requires a closer examination. A determination in the judicial system, if not action by the legislative or executive branches, is required to correctly delineate the status of this program, which has become abusive of the current system and, more important, abusive of the basic human rights of individuals.

Our fellow officers on active duty face a different situation altogether. They have fewer options but the same responsibility to use the appropriate chain of command to express their concerns and receive valid responses. Some orders must be questioned. Insanity ruled in Vietnam when Lieutenant Calley's orders were followed, killing between 300 and 400 unarmed Vietnamese women and children at My Lai. Insanity reigned in the AVIP when an illegally licensed vaccine was used for a purpose it was never intended and began producing friendly-fire victims. The victim count will increase until someone has the courage to defend basic human rights at home as we do abroad. Power behind the syringe is being abused, just as power behind a rifle was at My Lai, to violate basic human rights, international and federal law, personal legal rights, constitutional freedoms, and ethical standards of conduct.

Obviously, all orders cannot be questioned while still maintaining good order and discipline, which is what most commanders feared with anthrax refusers. The check on the abuse of power is a privilege of enormous responsibility, which itself must not be abused. But to ensure accountability and legal and moral compliance, military officers must have that freedom and the wisdom to use the chain of command to dutifully question the legality of orders, when necessary. History proves the use of this check to be the exception rather than the rule, but a necessary exception at that.

In 1805, British Admiral Lord Horatio Nelson won the most decisive naval victory of the nineteenth century at Trafalgar, after not "seeing" his commander's signal to "discontinue (the) engagement." He later explained, "I have only one eye; I have a right to be blind sometimes." In 1914, at Tannenberg, German corps commander General Hermann von Francois repeatedly disobeyed orders. He ended up capturing 90,000 prisoners, destroying a complete Russian army, and winning a major victory.[37]

The battle against the AVIP is one that had to be fought to protect future abuses, especially in light of JVAP, to protect the rule of law and basic human rights and to prevent future victims. Members of the U.S. Army, Navy, Air Force, Marines, and National Guard call themselves the "walking dead," because they don't know if or when they may become disabled in the long run because of the AVIP.

Blind obedience to a program or a person, even if he is the commander in chief, to protect one's own family, financial, and job security is not what the Oath of Office requires. Extreme care must be taken on delicate issues, but apathy is the other extreme. Passive acquiescence is the widespread response and has allowed this unbelievable program to thrive.

AVIP is still here, and time is running out.

CHAPTER 7

The Time Is Now

Justice is truth in action.

—Benjamin Disraeli

Failure is the opportunity to begin again, more intelligently.

—Henry Ford

The credit belongs to those who are actually in the arena, who strive valiantly; who know the great enthusiasm, the great devotions, and spend themselves in a worthy cause; who at the best, know the triumph of high achievement; and who, at the worst, if they fail, fail while daring greatly, so that their place shall never be with those cold and timid souls who know neither victory nor defeat.

—Theodore Roosevelt

An Uncontrolled Vaccine

It's getting worse, not better.

What started out as disbelief and skepticism (surely our own government wouldn't harm the very forces we rely on for protection!) has escalated into outrage, as AVIP spins out of control and more evidence is stacked against the vaccine.

Unfortunately, the outrage seems to have had little impact on the quality, standards, infrastructure, or methodology of the AVIP or its supporting players. Even now, when you can read volumes of reports condemning the vaccine, and then hear the same story when you view the Web sites, read the newspapers, watch the details on the evening news, and hear firsthand accounts from the victims, the AVIP lives on, and BioPort is still the vaccine manufacturer of choice.

It's not just frightening; it's absurd.

As this book goes to press, BioPort has just gained its approval from the FDA to reopen its manufacturing facility and resume production of the anthrax vaccine. FDA changed the labeling to include stronger and more specific warnings, an admission that the vaccine has serious flaws. Birth defects are the latest "minor side effect" that is being studied, and meanwhile, Dr. William Winkenwerder, Jr., assistant secretary of defense for health affairs, asked the [armed] services to devise a way to enhance the screening of women of childbearing age, "potentially including pregnancy testing," to prevent pregnant women from getting the vaccine.[1]

The reopening of BioPort is a mixed blessing. Even though one incident after another has pointed to BioPort's failures, the critical issues surrounding the anthrax vaccine are now in the spotlight, emerging with an urgency that will hopefully spur more people to awareness and action.

You might see this headline next: "BioPort Loses Truckload of Anthrax Vaccine." The company recently tried to solve one of its problems—the existence of gasket material in the vaccine—by hiring Hollister-Stier Laboratories LLC of Spokane, Washington, to perform the task of filling the vials of anthrax vaccine. A truck was filled with the anthrax vaccine at BioPort in Michigan and sent off to the West Coast.

Although yet unconfirmed, an undisclosed source reports that when the truck arrived in Spokane, it was empty.

Were transporting, delivery, storage, and security on the FDA's approval checklist?

Was the vaccine stolen? You've already seen in chapter 3 that security surrounding the anthrax vaccine has been lax. The implication that vaccine would be stolen for experimental research—or for protection during an anthrax attack—is not farfetched.

Did it leak its way across the country? The consequences of leakage could be monumental if the vaccine contained bovine-derived materials, especially since medical experts are not convinced that BioPort was truly producing a dead vaccine. Even though we are still waiting to confirm that this incident occurred, none of us would be surprised if it did.

On September 4, 2000, lawyers for BioPort requested the state government's help in retrieving missing documents containing the recipe for the anthrax vaccine. Why didn't BioPort have the recipe? The documents are at the center of a dispute with three former state scientists who want royalties for their work on the vaccine. Take the unspecified elements and contaminants in the vaccine, add a missing recipe, and anyone would conclude that this program should have been put out to pasture a long time ago.

Exploring that pasture may find us the elusive recipe. "Choose your cows carefully" may become the new motto of the AVIP. Remember mad cow disease and the horrifying losses that Europe has experienced? It seems that BioPort irked the FDA further by disregarding the FDA's 1993 and 1996 directives to stop using the bovine-derived materials of unknown geographic origin found in BioPort's anthrax vaccine. You can add mad cow disease to your aggravation about this vaccine, because BioPort was still using bovine-derived material in March 2001. According to recent research, the BioPort-induced threat of mad cow disease may be closer than we think.[2]

In fact, BioPort has had difficulty just trying to produce vaccine with the same consistency and the same potency twice in a row, yet now it appears that the FDA is suddenly comfortable with BioPort's performance. Health and Human Services Secretary Tommy Thompson predicts that within a month of FDA's authorization to reopen BioPort, the facility could be producing 80,000 more vaccines a week. That means this hazardous vaccine will be available again soon, and either the AVIP or the JVAP will be in force. Time is running out for the military, and the public has still not been provided accurate information about the effects of the vaccine.

Although it may seem a good thing that the amount of vaccine has diminished to about 24,000 doses (as of November 2001), it has actually intensified the military's urgency to produce more vaccine. Almost 6 million doses are in quarantine, and the fear is that these doses will be released if there are more terrorist attacks. Now that BioPort has been approved, the FDA says, "Three batches of previously produced vaccine have passed quality checks and can be shipped immediately."[3]

The JVAP provides more pressure. A National Security Research Council study released in June 2001 recommended that the Army embrace biotechnology and seek exemptions from regulatory approval processes to speed up the development of medical treatments. The council seems to envision a soldier with increased strength and superior resistance to disease and aging, a "Robo-soldier," and suggests that the Army seek means of sidestepping the FDA. "How can we ensure safety of the troops if we have to go through an onerous two or five years of certification?" asked Robert Lowe, National Academy of Sciences study director.[4] History is full of examples of moral and legal rights abused in the name of expediency, convenience, and greed. It will take more than an indifferent, uninformed public to stop this pattern.

Apathy is a common American attitude. Personally and professionally, I could not renounce my duty as a supervisor and commander. I was offered an easy out—the anonymous status of retirement—but I could not in good faith turn away from helpless victims and subordinates who did not have a voice. And, while I was not itching to get involved in this AVIP mess, I could not shirk my responsibility of command. I took the lonely position of a commander standing up for his troops against overwhelming odds to question and fight the AVIP.

Throughout all this, we get the disturbing feeling that there is an undercurrent, a series of connections that neither the armed forces nor the public are allowed to know.

For example, in a *CNN Morning News* interview on May 31, 1999, Senator Don Riegle, stated, "He [Saddam Hussein] got those biological and chemical weapons, the things to make them from the U.S. in the first place."[5] Earlier that year, congressional investigators learned that in the 1980s, the American Type Culture Company from Rockville, Maryland, which sells microbes to scientists, shipped, with government approval, up to thirty-six strains of deadly pathogens to Iraq. Some had come from Fort Detrick. Iraq imported about forty tons of biological growth media, thirty times more than was needed for civilian use. After weapons inspections in 1995, seventeen tons were missing and unaccounted for.[6]

Another example comes from a Chicago-based investigative reporter, Sherman Skolnick. He wrote in November 2001 that "investment firms tied to former President George H.W. Bush, such as the Carlyle Group, located six blocks from the White House on Pennsylvania Avenue, and the bin Laden family have invested in BioPort."[7]

Sometimes unmasking the truth has unsettling revelations that demand action.

As U.S. citizens under our Constitution, you can make a difference. With information comes responsibility. It's not enough to know; we must act on what we know. Whether you're a housewife or working for the CIA to prevent the next terrorist attack, you have the ability to respond, or "response-ability." It's not a privilege; it's your right. The consequence of inaction is the unacceptable situation at hand.

Let's care for those who have been injured. Let's stir our hearts to action and find no lack of courage. Let's make things right, for the rights and liberty of all who follow us, both here and abroad. Let's make a difference and repay the many who have sacrificed so much. Let's make it true in our lifetime. Let's strive once more to those high ideals.

Remember the courage in action on September 11. As United Flight 93 crash victim Todd Beamer said before his heroic attempt to save the lives of innocent people: "Let's roll!"

APPENDIX

Recommendations

Courage is the first quality of a warrior.
                                —Karl von Clausewitz

Recommendations for the Government

- Stop the current AVIP immediately.

- Require a waiver of informed consent, if the AVIP continues.

- Require FDA certification and regulatory compliance by BioPort, if the AVIP continues.

- Restore all victims hurt physically, medically, or professionally from the AVIP.

- Provide AVIP amnesty, correct all military records of service members punished, discharged, forced to resign or transfer, or court-martialed for opposing the AVIP.

- Compensate financially for all fines, legal costs, garnished wages, and medical bills of those injured by the AVIP.

- Research anthrax to provide a better vaccine immediately from multiple competing industry sources.

- Establish independent, civilian medical oversight for the Defense Department practice of medicine.

- Provide safeguards to prevent the JVAP from going the same road as the AVIP by ensuring vaccines are developed, tested, approved, and licensed to remain within legal and ethical guidelines.

- Provide for FDA responsibility of regulation of vaccines. Force the Defense Department, the FDA, and the AVIP, if continued, to comply with existing U.S. laws.

- Initiate a Department of Justice investigation of Defense Department and FDA officials responsible for the AVIP, especially those who have misled Congress or violated laws on informed consent.

- Require full financial disclosure and investigation of all BioPort and Defense Department employees involved with the AVIP during the last few years

- Pursue better, stronger, verifiable, and enforceable biological warfare treaties.

- Pursue safer, legal, ethical, effective, and doctrinally sound alternatives of force protection.

Recommendations for You

■ Get involved. You could be next.

■ Get more informed. Do your own research. This book is only one of a growing number of resources that provide accurate and up-to-date accounts of the medical, military and public aspects of the anthrax vaccine. Start by looking into these Web sites:

www.majorbates.com

www.anthraxvaccine.org

www.anthraxvaccine.net

www.gulflink.org

www.gulfwarvets.com

www.house.gov/reform/ns/reports/anthraxreport.pdf

www.house.gov/reform/ns/reports/anthrax1.pdf

www.dallasnw.quik.com/cyberella

www.dallasnw.quik.com/cyberella/Anthrax/Chron_Info.html

www.jamesmadisonproject.org/anthraxpage.html

www.enter.net/~jfsorg

www.tomcolosimo.com

■ Spread the word. Inform your friends and family who are in the military and any others who may be at risk.

■ Call or e-mail your representatives in Congress today. Remember: It takes only twelve calls to highlight an issue for a member of Congress, and to send the message of grave concern on the part of constituents.

Notes

Introduction

1. Redmond Handy, "Analysis of DOD's Anthrax Vaccine Immunization Program (AVIP)," report presented at the Call for Amnesty Press Conference, Washington D.C., February 12, 2001, p. 2.

2. Statement by Kathryn C. Zoon, Ph. D., Director, Center for Biologics Evaluation and Research Food and Drug Administration, Department of Human Services, *Hearing before the Subcommittee on National Security, Veterans Affairs, and International Relations, Committee on Government Reform, U.S. House of Representatives on April 29, 1999*, (Washington D.C.) p. 2.

3. Statement by Kwai Chan, *Hearing before the Subcommittee on National Security, Veterans Affairs, and International Relations, Committee on Government Reform, U.S. House of Representatives on May 7, 1999*, (Washington D.C.) p. 2.

Chapter 1

1. Thomas Paine, from his essay, *The American Crisis,* 1776.

2. The 1994 Rockefeller Report Examining Biological Experimentation on U.S. Military, Washington, D.C.

3. Catherine Unwin, et.al., "Health of UK Servicemen Who Served in the Persian Gulf War," *The Lancet,* January 16, 1999, p. 169.

4. Fulco, Carolyn E., Catharyn T. Liverman, Harold C. Sox, eds., Institute of Medicine, "Gulf War and Health: Volume 1. Depleted Uranium, Sarin, Pyridostigmine Bromide," *Vaccines,* Washington, DC: National Academy Press, 2000, p. 1-5, 14-18.

5. Statement by Chan, p. 4.

6. Thomas L. Rempfer and Russ Dingle, "Information Paper for America's Policy Makers," W. Suffield, CT, October 26, 1999, p. 7.

7. Ibid.

8. Meryl Nass, MD, "Dissecting Propaganda: Dr. Poland Supports the AVIP," February 7, 2000, p. 5.

9. Ibid., p. 6.

10. Thomas D. Williams, "Report Offers No Answer on Anthrax Vaccine Safety," *Hartford Courant,* July 3, 2001.

11. James Merriweather, "Anthrax Shots Stop at DAFB," *TheNewsJournal,* Dover, Delaware, August 29, 1999.

12. Thomas D. Williams, "Report Offers No Answer on Anthrax Vaccine Safety," *Hartford Courant,* July 3, 2001.

13. Emily Kelley, "Anthrax Vaccine Recipients Report Ailments," *Stars and Stripes,* October 6, 2000.

14. Redmond Handy, Briefing Slide, "Systemic Reaction Levels for 2.5 Million Service Members Based on Various DOD Quotes," May 12, 1999.

15. Statement by Chan, p. 3.

16. Handy, "Analysis," p. 7.

17. William F. Jasper, "Vexing Vaccine," *New American,* Vol. 16, No. 24, November, 20, 2000, p. 10.

18. Nass, "Dissecting Propaganda," p. 13.

19. Meryl Nass, MD, "Anthrax Vaccine: A Model Response to the Threat of Biological Warfare," July 19, 1998, p. 14.

20. Statement by Zoon, p. 3-4.

21. Nass, "Dissecting Propaganda," p. 7.

22. Handy, "Analysis," p. 7.

23. Ibid.

24. Nass, "Dissecting Propaganda," p. 9.

25. Tom Mangold and Jeff Goldberg, *Plague Wars,* St. Martin's Press, Inc., March 2001.

26. Statement by Chan, p. 5.

27. House Committee on Government Reform report, *Unproven Force Protection,* February 17, 2000, p. 3.

28. Handy, "Analysis," p. 12.

Chapter 2

1. Laura Johannes and Mark Maremont, "Injecting Doubt: Worries About Safety of Its Anthrax Vaccine Put the Army in a Bind," *The Wall Street Journal,* p. A1, October 12, 2001.

2. Kent Miller, "What the Government Doesn't Want You to Know About the Anthrax Vaccine," Letter to the Editor, *Air Force Times,* April/May 2001.

3. Brachman and Friedlander, *Anthrax,* 1994, in Plotkin SA and Mortimer EA Jr. (eds): *Vaccines,* ed 2., Philadelphia, WB Saunders, 1994, p. 729-739.

4. Nass, "Dissecting Propaganda," p. 9.

5. USAMRIID Briefing Slide, p.5.

6. Wayne Wilson, "Reservists Criticize Anthrax Shots," Bee Staff Writer, March 20, 2000.

7. Meryl Nass MD, NSVAIR Anthrax Hearing (II) p. 102, House Report, p. 38.

8. Jasper, "Vexing Vaccine," p. 10.

9. Statement by Zoon, p. 7.

10. Handy, "Analysis," p. 14.

11. Kate House, "Survey Indicates Wide Variety of Reactions to Anthrax Vaccination," *Dover Post*, March 14, 2000.

12. Major Sonnie G. Bates, Memorandum for Brigadier General Starbuck, "Response to Article 15 Proceedings," February 21, 2000, Attachment.

13. Elaine M. Grossman, "Institute Finds 'Paucity' Of Research On Anthrax Vaccine Safety," *Inside the Pentagon*, April 13, 2000.

14. Handy, "Analysis," p. 8.

15. LTG Ronald Blanck, U.S. Army Surgeon General, letter to the editor, *Washington Times*, March 14, 2000.

16. Disabled American Veterans' Candidate Forum, April 2000.

17. Unwin, et.al., "Health of UK Servicemen," p. 169.

18. Stephen E. Straus, "Commentary," *The Lancet*, January 16, 1999, p. 162.

19. Charles Miller, "Reserve Troops Suffering From Syndrome," *PA News*, September 24, 1997.

20. Dr. Lea Steele, epidemiologist and Senior Health Researcher, Kansas Health Institute, 1997.

21. Ibid.

22. Meryl Nass, MD, "Anthrax Vaccine Safety and Efficacy," response to General Blanck's posting, May 4, 1998.

23. Ibid.

24. Ibid.

25. Gary Matsumoto, "The Pentagon's Toxic Secret," *Vanity Fair*, May 1999, p. 88.

26. Ibid., page 90.

27. Viera Scheibner, Ph.D., Adjuvants, "Preservatives and Tissue Fixatives in Vaccines," *Nexus*, December 2000 (Vol 8, No1).

28. Gary Matsumoto, "The Pentagon's Toxic Secret," *Vanity Fair,* May 1999, p. 94.

29. Jeff J., C-141 pilot/Memphis/Federal Express interview with Dr. Pam Asa, e-mail April 28, 1999, p. 3.

30. Kathryn C. Zoon, Ph.D., Director, Center for Biologics Evaluation and Research, Letter to Robert Myers, D.V.M., March 11, 1997.

31. *Anthrax Vaccine Stockpile Overview,* Report Date July 15, 1998.

32. Statement by Zoon, p. 9.

33. "Anthrax Vaccine Report Shows Spikes in Potency," *San Francisco Chronicle,* November 2, 2001.

34. Meryl Nass MD, NSVAIR Anthrax Hearing (II) p. 102, House Report, Blumenthal Letter, p. 8.

35. Dave Eberhart, "Anthrax Vaccine? No, Not Yet," *NewsMax.com,* October 29, 2001.

36. Laura Johannes and Mark Maremont, "Injecting Doubt: Worries About Safety of Its Anthrax Vaccine Put the Army in a Bind," *The Wall Street Journal,* p. A1, October 12, 2001.

Chapter 3

1. Dave Eberhart, "DOD Anthrax Documents and E-Mails Bolster Buck's Unlawful Order Defense," Army Times Publishing Co. Pentagon Newspaper, *The Early Bird,* May 15, 2001.

2. Congressman Jack Metcalf, letter to Secretary of Defense William Cohen, Washington, D.C., May 16, 2000.

3. Statement by Chan, p. 2.

4. U.S. Department of State, Washington, D.C., "FACT SHEET: Chemical - Biological Agents", http://travel.state.gov/cbw.html.

5. DARPA Briefing Slide.

6. George Bush and Brent Scowcroft, *A World Transformed,* Random House, 1998, p. 441-442.

7. Meryl Nass MD, "Anthrax Vaccine and the Prevention of Biological Warfare," p. 6.

8. "An Unlikely Threat and Bad Medicine for Biological Terror," *Bulletin of the Atomic Scientists,* Nov/Dec 1999.

9. Nass, "Dissecting Propaganda," p. 3.

10. Handy, "Analysis," p. 55.

11. Ibid., p. 46.

12. William M. Arkin, "The Man Who Never Was," *Washington Post.com,* January 29, 2001.

13. William S. Cohen, "Preparing for a Grave New World," *Washington Post,* July 26, 1999.

14. Handy, "Analysis," p. 49.

15. Thomas D. Williams, "Anthrax Vaccine Deal Criticized," *Hartford Courant,* August 13, 1999.

16. Jack Dolan and Dave Altimari, "Anthrax Missing from Army Lab", *Hartford Courant,* January 20, 2002.

17. Lynne Tuohy and Jack Dolan, "Turmoil in a Perilous Place", *Hartford Courant,* December 19, 2001.

18. Handy, "Analysis," p. 49.

19. Nicholas Wade, "Tests With Anthrax Raise Fears That American Vaccine Can Be Defeated," *The New York Times National,* March 26, 1998.

20. Interview with Dr. Ken Alibek, reprinted by Thomas Rempfer, e-mail, September 14, 1999.

21. Dr. Ken Alibek in statement to Joint Economic Committee of Congress on May 20, 1998.

22. Handy, "Analysis," p. 18.

23. Meryl Nass MD, "Anthrax Vaccine Safety and Efficacy," response to General Blanck's posting, May 4, 1998.

24. Handy, "Analysis," p. 9.

25. Statement by Chan, p. 4.

26. Meryl Nass MD, "Anthrax Vaccine Safety and Efficacy," response to General Blanck's posting, May 4, 1998.

27. SAIC Slide Briefing, "Anthrax Vaccine License, Amendment Project Plan," October 19, 1995, p. 5.

28. Nicholas Regush, "Will the Vaccine Work?," ABC News.com, October 8, 2001.

29. Redmond Handy, Briefing Slide, "1998 Ft. Detrick Guinea Pig Study," April 22, 1999.

30. Nass, "Dissecting Propaganda," p. 11.

31. Meryl Nass, MD, "Concerns Regarding Announced Anthrax

Vaccinations: Lack of Demonstrated Safety and Efficacy," a ProMED-mail post, January 2, 1998.

32. Dave Eberhart, "Anthrax Vaccine? No, Not Yet," *NewsMax.com,* October 29, 2001.

33. Handy, "Analysis," p. 47.

Chapter 4

1. Jennifer Martin, "Air Guard Steps Up For Anthrax Vaccine," *Indianapolis Star,* January 10, 2000.

2. Dave Eberhart, "General's Anthrax Vaccine Testimony 'Inconsistent With Honesty' Says Inspector," *Stars and Stripes,* May 11, 2001.

3. General John D. Ryan, "Air Force Policy Letter for Commanders, Washington, D.C., November 1, 1972.

4. VHS Tape #2, Closed-circuit TV Warrior Broadcast by Director of the ANG on AVIP.

5. Colonel James Dougherty, Surgeon General of the National Guard Bureau, in testimony to Congressional hearing, Government Reform Subcommittee, House of Representatives.

6. GAO Report, "Anthrax Vaccine Preliminary Results of GAO Survey of Guard/Reserve Pilots and Aircrew Members, October 11, 2000.

7. Mark S. Zaid, Executive Director, The James Madison Project, in testimony to House Government Reform Subcommittee, March 24, 1999, p. 17.

Chapter 5

1. Dave Eberhart, "Air Force Balks At Buck Resignation; Anthrax Trial Continues," *Stars and Stripes,* May 21, 2001.

2. Thomas D. Williams, "Doctors Vs. Anthrax Vaccine," *Hartford Courant,* May 14, 2001.

3. Thomas D. Williams, "Air Force Will Not Let Doctor Resign," *Hartford Courant,* May 19, 2001.

4. General Ronald Blanck, in testimony to Senate Armed Services Committee, April 13, 2000.

5. Handy, "Analysis," p. 3.

6. Ibid.

7. Robert Maginnis, "Distrust Corroding the Military," *Washington Times,* March 2, 2000.

8. Mark S. Zaid, Executive Director, The James Madison Project, in testimony to House Government Reform Subcommittee, March 24, 1999, p. 28.

9. http://www.anthrax.osd.mil/, June through October 1999.

10. Thomas D. Williams, "E-Mails Suggest Pentagon Pressured FDA on Anthrax Vaccine," *Hartford Courant,* May 17, 2001.

11. Ibid.

12. Dave Eberhart, "DOD Anthrax Documents and E-Mails Bolster Buck's Unlawful Order Defense," Army Times Publishing Co. Pentagon Newspaper, *The Early Bird,* May 15, 2001.

13. Handy, "Analysis," p. 2.

14. Ibid., p. 11.

15. Ibid., p. 57.

16. Keith J. Costa, "Audit Paints 'Bleak Picture' Of Anthrax Vaccine Maker's Viability", *Inside the Pentagon,* April 13, 2000, p. 14.

17. David Oppliger (3-4827), House Majority Counsel to Democratic Members of the House Oversight and Ethics Committee, September 23, 1998, p. 4.

18. Ibid., p. 1.

19. Ibid., p. 2.

20. Dave Eberhart, "Anthrax Vaccine Maker Didn't Report Army Sergeant's Death, According to FDA," *Stars and Stripes,* March 6, 2001.

21. William F. Jasper, "Vexing Vaccine," *New American,* Vol. 16, No. 24, November, 20, 2000.

22. Christopher Boliyn, "Only U.S. Anthrax Vaccine Maker Called Negligent," *American Free Press,* November 8, 2001.

23. Keith J. Costa, "Audit Paints 'Bleak Picture' Of Anthrax Vaccine Maker's Viability", *Inside the Pentagon,* April 13, 2000, p. 14.

Chapter 6

1. House Armed Services Committee Hearing, Personnel Subcommittee, October 12, 2000.

2. Representative Steve Buyer, "Anthrax Vaccine Supporter Loses District in 2002," *USA Today,* April 12, 2001, p. 11A.

3. Interview with Representative Steve Buyer, with "Charlie" transmitted by e-mail from Thomas Rempfer, January 10, 2000.

4. Nicholas Regush, "Can We Get Serious About the Problems With the Anthrax Vaccine," *ABC News Commentary,* October 11, 2001.

5. Howard Urnovitz, Testimony to the Subcommittee on National Security, Veterans' Affairs and International Relations, U.S. House of Representatives, Committee on Government Reform, January 24, 2002, p. 2.

6. Thomas Rempfer, Information Paper, p. 7.

7. Statement by Zoon, p. 2.

8. George J. Annas, "Protecting Soldiers from Friendly Fire: The Consent Requirement for Using Investigational Drugs and Vaccines in Combat," *American Journal of Law and Medicine,* Vol. XXIV, Nos. 2 & 3, 1998, p. 252.

9. Ibid., p. 257.

10. Ibid., p. 247.

11. Timothy W. Maier, "Clinton Orders Human Experiments," *Insight Magazine,* October 22, 1999.

12. William F. Jasper, "Vexing Vaccine," *New American,* Vol. 16, No. 24, November, 20, 2000, p. 8.

13. Attorney General Richard Blumenthal, letter to Secretary of Defense Rumsfeld, March 22, 2001, p. 4-10.

14. Ibid., p. 11.

15. Meryl Nass MD, "Anthrax Vaccine Safety and Efficacy," response to General Blanck's posting, May 4, 1998, p. 4.

16. The 1994 Rockefeller Report, "Examining Biological Experimentation on U.S. Military."

17. Ibid.

18. Handy, "Analysis," p. 9.

19. Attorney General Richard Blumenthal, letter to Secretary of Defense Rumsfeld, March 22, 2001, p. 6.

20. Handy, "Analysis," p. 16.

21. Ibid., p. 9.

22. Ibid., p. 24.

23. Ibid., p. 26.

24. Ibid., p. 27.

25. *FoxNews Report,* "FDA Silent on 'Illegal' Anthrax Vaccine in U.S. Study," December 18, 2001.

26. Ibid.

27. Ibid.

28. Ibid.

29. Ibid.

30. Ibid.

31. Statement by Zoon, p. 4-5.

32. Harold E. Hughes, former Senator, Iowa, Congressional Record - U.S. Senate, 1974:56258.

33. Huntington, "The Soldier and the State," Cambridge, MA, Belnap Press of Harvard University Press, copyright © 1957 by the President and Fellows of Harvard College.

34. Malham M. Wakin, United States Air Force Academy, "The Ethics of Leadership", *American Behaviorial Scientist,* Vol. 19, No. 5, May/June 1976.

35. Ibid.

36. Ibid.

37. David H. Hackworth, Defending America: "Lap Dogs or Tigers?", December 2, 1999.

Chapter 7

1. Associated Press, "New safety concerns on anthrax shots," January 17, 2002.

2. Center for Biologics Evaluation and Research, "MMWR Notice to Readers: PHS Recommendations for the Use of Vaccines Manufactured with Bovine-Derived Materials."

3. Associated Press, "Anthrax vaccine maker gets FDA OK," February 1, 2002.

4. UPI Newsservice, Washington, D.C., June 20, 2001.

5. *CNN Morning News,* May 31, 1999.

6. William J. Broad and Judith Miller, "How Iraq's Biological Weapons Program Came to Light," *New York Times on the Web,* February 26, 1998.

7. Boliyn, "Only U.S. Anthrax Vaccine Maker."